# Praise for The Key

"For those of us who loved *The Attractor Factor* and *The Secret*, Joe has done it again. *The Key* is the how-to book that makes the 'law of attraction' come alive!"
   —Jessica Biel, actor and philanthropist

"Joe Vitale's energy and enthusiasm for life jumps off every page of his new book, *The Key*. He leaves no stone unturned in explaining exactly how to attract everything you want in your life. The words 'I love you' have taken on a whole new meaning. Bravo!"
   —Cathy Lee Crosby, actress and author of *Let the Magic Begin*

"Joe Vitale reveals the hidden 'obstacles' behind most failed attempts at manifestation and attraction. If you have been unable to manifest or attract what you truly desire, the missing secret he outlines in this book will open the door for you. Knowing and applying this key in your life will more than pay for the cost of this book! Read it and reap the benefits!"
   —Dr. Robert Anthony, author of *Beyond Positive Thinking*
      www.drrobertanthony.com

"This is one of the most powerful resources I have ever read! *The Key* is completely life-transforming, brilliantly simple, and can unlock the door to everything you desire. This book ranks up there with the classics."
   —Peggy McColl, author of *Your Destiny Switch*
      www.destinyswitch.com

"*The Key* has been a secret for far too long. Joe Vitale shows us how to easily and precisely unlock the conscious and unconscious impediments to our success and clear the way to unlimited self-improvement. This is a must-read for all!"
   —Dr. R. F. Barrett, wellness advisor and author of *Dare to Break Through the Pain*
      www.2healnow.com

"In his typically engaging storytelling style, Joe Vitale addresses the toughest questions and objections related to manifesting your desires. Further, he provides a remarkable collection of tools to help you eliminate even the most stubborn blocks and limiting beliefs, thus clearing the way for any and all possibilities. An absolute must-read for anyone serious about living their life by design."
   —Bob Doyle, creator and facilitator of the Wealth Beyond Reason program
      www.wealthbeyondreason.com

# The Key

*The Key*

# The Missing Secret for Attracting Anything You Want

## JOE VITALE

John Wiley & Sons, Inc.

Published by John Wiley & Sons, Inc., Hoboken, New Jersey.
Published simultaneously in Canada.

Wiley Bicentennial Logo: Richard J. Pacifico

For general information on our other products and services or for technical support, please contact our Customer Care Department within the United States at (800) 762-2974, outside the United States at (317) 572-3993 or fax (317) 572-4002.

Wiley also publishes its books in a variety of electronic formats. Some content that appears in print may not be available in electronic books. For more information about Wiley products, visit our web site at www.wiley.com.

*Library of Congress Cataloging-in-Publication Data:*

Vitale, Joe, 1953-
  The Key : the missing secret for attracting anything you want! / Joe Vitale.
    p. cm.
  Includes bibliographical references and index.
  ISBN 978-0-470-18076-1 (cloth : alk. paper)
 1. New Thought. 2. Success. 3. Conduct of life. I. Title.
  BF639.V58 2008
  158—dc22                                                                    2007024180

Printed in the United States of America.

10 9 8 7 6 5 4 3 2 1

*To Neville Goddard*

*You are the masterpiece of your own life; you are the Michelangelo of your own life. The David that you are sculpting is you.*

—Dr. Joe Vitale, from the movie *The Secret*

# Contents

## Part Three: The Miracles

# The Optimist Creed

**_Promise Yourself:_**

To be so strong that nothing can disturb your peace of mind.

To talk health, happiness, and prosperity to every person you meet.

To make all your friends feel that there is something in them.

To look at the sunny side of everything and make your optimism come true.

To think only of the best, to work only for the best, and to expect only the best.

To be just as enthusiastic about the success of others as you are about your own.

To forget the mistakes of the past and press on to the greater achievements of the future.

To wear a cheerful countenance at all times and give every living creature you meet a smile.

To give so much time to the improvement of yourself that you have no time to criticize others.

To be too large for worry, too noble for anger, too strong for fear, and too happy to permit the presence of trouble.

To think well of yourself and to proclaim this fact to the world, not in loud words but in great deeds.

To live in the faith that the whole world is on your side so long as you are true to the best that is in you.

Note: "The Optimist Creed" was first published in 1912 in Christian D. Larson's book, _Your Forces and How to Use Them_. A shortened version of it is used today by Optimist International, a worldwide group of people who are focused on making a positive difference in the world.

# Foreword

I want you to imagine a large lock. It's strong and very difficult to open. This lock is keeping you where you do not want to be. However, you seem to have an awareness that the lock will open and, if opened, you will feel and experience the freedom you have, until now, only been privileged to read about. You dream of living where you want to live, enjoying everything the way you were meant to enjoy it, earning the income you know deep inside you can earn, living the way you were intended to live, and contributing in a manner you know you should.

This is a powerful lock. Until opened, this lock keeps people in a psychic prison—a dark place that respects no one, a confining cell, a limiting space that kills dreams and keeps smart, loving, aspiring people down. This is indeed one of the most powerful locks. Can you see it? I think you can!

This is the lock that's within the mind of man; it is a paradigm.

The book you are now holding represents a way out . . . freedom. *The Key: The Missing Secret for Attracting Anything You Want* by Joe Vitale will open up a world of possibility and promise. It will answer your nagging questions as to why you don't yet have the abundance you know you should have and that you deserve. This book will give you serious, time-tested, and practical strategies to unlock that lock forever.

If you are looking for a book that explains how to make things happen in your life and you want to expand your awareness, I suggest that you adopt this book as a new and dear friend now. Devour it! But, most important, use it to unlock those places within yourself that have held you back.

For almost 40 years, I have been involved in helping individuals and companies the world over open that mysterious lock. I've read thousands of books on the subject and have spent over 40 years studying why we behave as we do. This book is an absolute must-read—cover to cover!

You see, I know Joe Vitale. I knew Joe when he was searching for the elusive Key. I observed him find it. I have watched his life and his world change. What is wonderful about Joe's discovery is how he has recorded every move. Like a great astronomer, Joe charted his moves so he can share these beautiful truths with you and everyone else who is tired of the psychic prison in which they may find themselves.

Joe Vitale is a widely respected teacher on how to unlock your hidden potential. I've read all of his books. This book, *The Key*, is likely to be considered his best. In his easy-to-read style, Joe unfolds what could be considered complex subjects and makes them easy to understand and, more important, easy to apply. He will challenge your thinking; that's what Joe is all about. He will make you think, laugh, and cry (possibly). But he will equip you to overcome the constraints of that ugly lock and open it.

Use this book as I suggested, and I promise you that strange and marvelous things will begin to happen in all areas of your life with constant regularity.

This is the book that will unlock a whole new world—it contains The Key.

—Bob Proctor
Best-selling author of *You Were Born Rich*
www.BobProctor.com

# Acknowledgments

As with every book I've ever written, many people supported and encouraged me in the writing process. Matt Holt, my dear friend and chief editor at John Wiley & Sons, is number one on the list. Without him, this book would remain only an idea. Nerissa, my life partner and love, is always there for me, and always feeding the critters so I can keep writing. I thank Rhonda Byrne, creator of the movie *The Secret*, for putting me in her amazing film so new people would hear of my work and want a book like this one. Suzanne Burns, my key assistant, makes my daily life easier so I can focus on writing.

Close friends gave me support and advice. They include Bill Hibbler, Pat O'Bryan, Jillian Coleman-Wheeler, Craig Perrine, and Cindy Cashman. My dear friend and fellow crusader of the light, Mark Ryan, is always supportive of my projects. Victoria Schaefer is totally supportive of me and my work, and is a priceless friend. I also want to thank Joe Sugarman, Howard Wills, Kathy Bolden, Marc Gitterle, Scott Lewis, Jeff Sargent, John Roper, Rick and Mary Barrett, Roopa and Deepak Chari, Will LaValley, Scott York, Mark Joyner, and Ann Taylor for their support of my well-being. In addition, I thank Cyndi Smasal and my Miracles Coaches team. Mark Weisser dropped everything in his busy schedule to edit the first draft of this book.

Finally, I'm grateful to the Divine for allowing me to do what I do. If I'm forgetting anyone, and I probably am, I apologize. I love you all.

# The Key

# Part One

## The Key

*Anybody who has been seriously engaged in scientific work of any kind realizes that over the entrance to the gates of the temple of science are written the words:*

*Ye must have faith.*

—Max Planck, winner of the 1918 Nobel prize in Physics

# The Missing Secret

*Beliefs are the determinant of what one experiences. There are no external causes.*

—David Hawkins, *I: Reality and Subjectivity*

Admit it. There is something in your life you've been trying to attract, achieve, or resolve and you simply haven't accomplished it yet.

It's not for lack of trying. You've read self-help books, seen movies such as *The Secret* and *What the Bleep Do We Know?*, attended seminars, and more. But you keep hitting your head against the wall when it comes to this one thing (or more) that you want and just can't seem to attract.

What gives? Why can you easily attract some things into your life but have a stubborn problem in this one area? Does the Law of Attraction really work or doesn't it? Does *anything* really work?

What's the missing secret to attracting whatever you want, anyway?

Everything in your life is there because you attracted it. This includes the bad stuff. You simply attracted it on an unconscious level. When you become aware of the mental programming that is operating behind your experiences, you can then change it and begin to attract what you prefer.

When you "get clear" (which I'll define shortly) of the hidden beliefs stopping you from attracting whatever you want, you get what others may call miracles. For example:

- When I got clear of the issues I had about being over-weight, I lost 80 pounds, entered six fitness contests, and transformed my body and my life.
- When I got clear of the hidden beliefs within myself regarding having a new car, I went on to attract 12 new ones, including now owning two BMWs and a stunning hand-assembled luxury sports car named Francine, a Panoz Esperante GTLM.
- When I got clear of why I created potentially deadly swollen lymph nodes in my chest, between my lungs, the nodes became harmless.
- When I got clear of why I was once homeless and then a struggling writer living in virtual poverty, I went on to become an Internet celebrity, a best-selling author of over 30 books, and one of the stars in a hit movie, *The Secret*.

Obviously, getting clear of your inner blocks is the missing secret to attracting whatever you want. How can you tell if you need to get clear right now? If you have to ask, you probably aren't clear. But here's a quick way to find out. Just truthfully answer these questions:

- Do you have a recurring problem area in your life?
- Have you ever set a New Year's resolution and not kept it?
- Are you frustrated by self-help methods that haven't worked for you?
- Are you not taking action to get what you want?

- Do you feel like something is sabotaging your success?
- Have you seen the movie *The Secret* and still not attracted what you want?

If you're completely honest with yourself, you know there is at least one area of your life that seems too stubborn to fix.

It may be in the area of weight loss. You've tried diets and you've exercised, and the weight either stays on or comes back on fast. You feel cursed.

It may be in relationships. You've tried dating, you've tried online services, you've been in relationships and maybe even married, but the love doesn't last. Something always happens to kill the romance.

Or finances. You've had jobs, and none of them fulfill you. Or you can't seem to find the right vocation for you, no matter how many guidance counselors you see and resumes you write. It just feels like the world isn't supporting you in going for your dreams. You're always broke or always trying to catch up with your bills.

Or health. Maybe you have a nagging backache, or something more challenging, like cancer or a muscular disease. Maybe it's an allergy, or a persistent cough, or asthma. Whatever it is, it feels like you can't heal it or cure it because you feel destined to have it.

The general feeling in every stuck issue is that you feel like a victim. You feel that the problem is yours but the cause is elsewhere. It's the fault of your boss, your neighbors, the president, the government, the terrorists, the pollution, global warming, your DNA, the IRS, or even God.

What's the solution?

What's The Key?

I've experienced this stuck feeling in my own life, when I was homeless and starving. I felt like the world was out to get me. I was angry at everyone, from my parents to the system, even to God. I didn't feel I deserved this life. Struggling to eat, then to find a place to live, then to find a car were agonizing and frustrating experiences. They certainly weren't my fault. I was a nice guy. I deserved better.

I had the same stuck experience in trying to lose weight. I was overweight as a child, as a teenager, and most of my adult life. I hated it. I blamed my parents for my body structure. I blamed them for how they raised me and how they fed me. I blamed my gym teachers for making me feel humiliated. I felt destined to stay fat, and I didn't like it one bit.

In both cases I had a recurring problem and didn't think I was the cause. I blamed outer circumstances. That's what most of us do when we hit a wall and can't get around it. It isn't us, we think; it's the wall. We might be successful in every other area of our lives, but when we come to this one stubborn area, we aren't clear and can't see our way out.

The point of this book is that there is a way out.

I call it The Key.

The Key is the missing secret to attracting whatever you want. I mean this in the most sincere way possible. It's the truth. It's reality. It's your ticket to freedom.

When I was homeless, I had to look at my own beliefs. I realized that the main reason I was unhappy and struggling was because I *expected* to be. I woke up to the idea that I was modeling my life on authors who had been suicidal. Since I wanted to be an author like they were, I thought being melancholy was the curriculum. Once I changed my beliefs, I began to attract a new reality. I began to get work, then money, then happiness. Today I am the author of dozens of books and I'm seen in such movies as *The Secret* and *The Opus*.

What happened to the stubborn problem that I blamed others for?

The same thing happened with my obesity. Today I'm average if not fit. I've been in six fitness contests. I built my own gym. I've trained with famous bodybuilders, such as Frank Zane.

What happened to my lifelong problem that I blamed my DNA for?

In both cases I used The Key to break free.

That's what this book is about. It's a manual on how to attract your wildest and most wonderful dreams—no matter what they may be.

All you need is The Key.

# The Key

*You unconsciously demand all your experiences, and you deliver to others the experiences they subconsciously request.*

—Susan Shumsky, *Miracle Prayer*

In the early 1900s, Wallace D. Wattles, author of *The Science of Getting Rich*, wrote the following in his rare, lesser-known essay, *How to Get What You Want*:

> People fail because they think, objectively, that they can do things, but do not know, subconsciously, that they can do them. It is more than likely that your subconscious mind is even now impressed with doubts of your ability to succeed; and these must be removed, or it will withhold its power when you need it most.

Wattles was hinting at The Key to attracting whatever you want. When your conscious mind thinks you want something but your subconscious thinks you don't deserve it (or any other limiting belief), you will fail at getting what you want. Instead, you will actually attract what you think you don't want. In reality, you will attract what your subconscious feels is right for you. In order to attract what you prefer, your conscious and subconscious have to be in agreement.

Susan Shumsky, in *Miracle Prayer*, wrote, "Your conscious beliefs are what you *think* you believe. Your subconscious beliefs and deepest convictions are what you *really* believe."

What you have in your life right now is what you wanted, at least unconsciously.

The Key is all about getting clear so your mind—both conscious and subconscious—is congruent. In my earlier book, *The

*Attractor Factor*, I listed getting clear as the third step in the formula for attracting miracles. So we are on the same page, let me review those five steps from that book:

1. Know what you don't want.
2. Choose what you do want.
3. Get clear.
4. Feel it already accomplished.
5. Let go while taking inspired action.

Those five steps will work for people in achieving their biggest goals and dreams. But if you practice the steps and feel blocked, or frustrated, and can't seem to manifest your goal no matter what, it may be because you are not completely clear. It may be because of an internal struggle: Part of you wants the goal but part of you doesn't. Your unconscious is vetoing your conscious desire.

Even people who have watched the movie *The Secret,* dozens and sometimes even hundreds of times, often still feel stuck in one area. That's because they have an inner opposing belief to their stated intention. Once you get clear of that limiting belief, results happen almost instantly.

The phrase "getting clear" means you get rid of the inner roadblocks to your own desires. I call these inner obstacles counter-intentions. The best way I know to understand counter-intentions is to think back to the last New Year's you remember.

Most likely you stated some New Year's resolutions. You said things like, "I'm going to work out every other day" or "I'm going to stop smoking" or "I'm going to make more money selling my art" or any number of things. You had the best intentions when you stated your goals. You fully expected to achieve them.

But what happened?

By the next day you may have forgotten where the gym is located. Or you're overeating again and have totally forgotten your resolution to improve your eating habits.

What happened is that your counter-intentions overrode your stated intentions.

Getting clear is removing the counter-intentions. When you do, you can have, do, or be anything you can imagine.

Getting clear is the missing secret to all self-help programs.

It's The Key to attracting whatever you want.

# How the Universe Works

*If you woke up this morning with more health than illness, you are more blessed than the million who will not survive the week.*

*If you have food in your refrigerator, clothes on your back, a roof over your head, and a place to sleep, you are richer than 75 percent of this world.*

*If you have money in the bank or in your wallet, you are among the top 8 percent of the world's wealthy.*

*If you hold up your head with a smile on your face and are truly thankful, you are blessed because the majority can, but most do not.*

—Author unknown

Have you ever received an idea for a product or service but didn't act on it? Maybe you got an idea for a new children's toy, or a new shampoo, or a new gizmo to help a certain group of people. Did you act on it? If you didn't, why not?

And let's look at the other side of the question. Have you ever asked the universe to do something for you but didn't get the result you requested? Did you ever visualize and not get what you imagined? If so, what happened?

In order to understand The Key, let me explain what happens between you and the universe.

1. The universe—call that huge superpower God, the Divine, Divinity, life, zero, Tao, or whatever works for you—is sending and receiving messages all the time. It's sending inspiration to you. It's receiving requests from you.
2. This dialogue is being filtered through your belief system, which causes you to take or not take actions.

3. The results you get are what happens from the first two steps. How you read those results is also based on your belief system.

As you can see from Figure 1 (created by Suzanne Burns), the universe (or the Divine, life, or any name that works for you to describe the nameless power), is ready to receive requests from you, and it's also trying to send messages to you. That communication gets filtered through your beliefs. The final result is what you call your reality. But if you change those beliefs, you'll get a different reality.

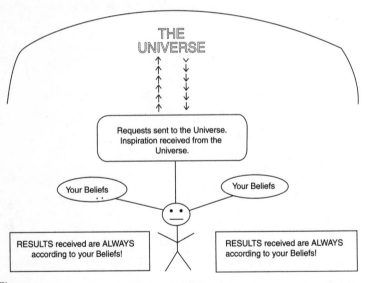

Figure 1.

For example, when you received an idea to create a new product, that idea came to you as a gift from the universe. But after you thought of the idea, you had judgments about it. Maybe you said things like, "But I don't know how to pull this off" or "But where will I get the money?" or "Surely someone else has already thought of this." All of those judgments and doubts were beliefs. And those beliefs stopped you from taking action. As a result, you didn't create the product.

In fact, you probably noticed later that someone else did. This is why I'm fond of saying, "The universe likes speed." The universe gives an idea for a new product or service to several people at the same time, knowing that most of them will talk themselves out of doing it. Success goes to those who take action.

But what about when you asked the universe for help? The universe is always there, ready to listen and fulfill. But often when it tries to help you, your own beliefs get in the way. For example, you may ask for a way to meet the ideal mate. The universe hears and tries to nudge you into joining a group where you could meet your ideal person. But you again talk yourself out of it, saying something like, "But I joined that group before" or "No one will ever want me because I'm too

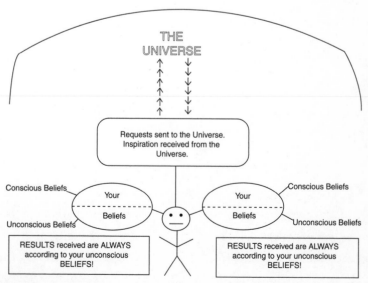

Figure 2.

(fill in the blank)." Once again, the universe is trying to help, but your own beliefs prevent it from succeeding.

It's important to understand that the beliefs operating in your world are most likely not conscious. You have conscious beliefs and you have unconscious or subconscious ones. The deeper ones are the more powerful. Those beliefs are the wiring that creates the programming operating your life. In order to get clear, you have to clean up those deeper beliefs. With that in mind, the way the universe works looks more like Figure 2.

In short, you live in a belief-created universe. To change your results, you have to change your *un*conscious beliefs. That's the area where you have to get clear. Again, getting clear is the missing secret to attracting whatever you want.

It's The Key.

# The Law of Attraction

*Nothing can stop the man with the right mental attitude from achieving his goal; nothing on earth can help the man with the wrong mental attitude.*

—Thomas Jefferson

Before you can understand The Key, you need to understand one of the lesser-known laws of the universe. When you are clear of all limiting beliefs within you, you consciously engage the Law of Attraction. You are already attracting everything into your life because of this law, but unconsciously.

This law was first formally introduced to the world in 1906. William Walker Atkinson described it in his book, *Thought Vibration, or The Law of Attraction in the Thought World.* In that book he wrote:

> We speak learnedly of the Law of Gravitation, but ignore that equally wonderful manifestation, THE LAW OF ATTRACTION IN THE THOUGHT WORLD. We are familiar with that wonderful manifestation of Law which draws and holds together the atoms of which matter is composed—we recognize the power of the law that attracts bodies to the earth, that holds the circling worlds in their places, but we close our eyes to *the mighty law that draws to us the things we desire or fear, that makes or mars our lives.*
>
> When we come to see that Thought is a force—a manifestation of energy—having a magnet-like power of attraction, we will begin to understand the why and wherefore of many things that have heretofore seemed dark to us. There is no study that will so well repay the student for his time and trouble as the study of the workings of this mighty law of the world of Thought—the Law of Attraction.

Today many people talk about this law. The Law of Attraction is described in the hit movie and book *The Secret*, and in my own book *The Attractor Factor*. It is taught by my dear friends Jerry and Esther Hicks in such books as *The Law of Attraction*. It is the fundamental law of psychology that says you get more of whatever you focus on. The thing is, most people are focused on what they don't want. As a result, they get more of it.

There are no exceptions to this law. I know you want there to be. But there aren't. Everything in your life was drawn to you because of the Law of Attraction. If this is a true law, and it is, then obviously there are no exceptions. None.

Let me explain with a personal story.

At the end of January 2007, I felt stomach pain. I ended up in the emergency room, and then having surgery for appendicitis. I recovered easily and quickly. But a reader of my books sent me this e-mail:

> Well, I'm sorry to hear about your appendicitis, but I'm really perplexed—how can the genius who wrote *The Attractor Factor* attract such a drastic experience??? According to your teaching, you DID attract it, but why?? I suppose you must have slipped up somewhere. . . . I hope you explain it to us, when you discover your mistake, so we can avoid similar consequences.

It was an honest question. I decided to answer it. Here's what I wrote back to her:

> Here's how I see it:
> Yes, I attracted this.
> We attract all of life.
> No exceptions.

The thing is, we attract it unconsciously.

We have no idea what we're doing, consciously. We're pretty much bumbling through life.

Myself included.

When doing research for my next book, *Zero Limits*, I discovered that our conscious mind isn't aware of much more than 15 bits of information in any one moment. The unconscious, however, is aware of billions of bits of information. Our larger operating system is obviously the unconscious.

The point of life is to awaken. To become fully conscious. We want to clean the unconscious of all limiting or negative programming so we can be in the divine flow that brings us magic and miracles.

But how do you do that?

In mid-January I co-led an intense and life-altering weekend called Zero Limits. It's based on the forthcoming book, *Zero Limits*. Dr. Ihaleakala Hew Len did most of the talking and led the adventure into our soul. The entire focus was on cleansing ourselves of what blocks us from our connection to source.

What I discovered is that there is an *unimaginably huge* amount of cleansing for all of us to do, myself included.

But I did the cleansing, and am still doing it.

After that historic weekend, my main computer stopped working.

So did my laptop.

And all my main sites, stemming from www.mrfire.com, went off-line.

Nothing was connected and yet all broke down the same weekend.

At that very same time I began to feel stomach problems.

By last Monday night, I was on the way to the emergency room to have my throbbing appendix removed.

What happened?

I'd say my body and life were being cleaned of everything weak or not working.

I'd also say it was an enforced vacation.

As Nerissa pointed out, I have been going and blowing at warp speed, taking on numerous projects, traveling, and barely (okay, never) stopping to relax and refresh.

My unconscious decided to stop me. By stopping my computers, and then me, it made me go on vacation.

But that's not the really important part of this story.

**Now please get this:**

I didn't see the experience—any of it—as negative.

I was never angry, upset, fearful, or had any other negative emotion.

I was at best curious.

I saw the unfolding of these events like an interactive movie with me the star player.

Believe me, I wouldn't wish an emergency appendectomy on anyone, but this was not the "drastic" experience you might imagine it to be.

Throughout it all, I kept saying "I love you" and the other cleaning phrases (see cleaning method #5).

I simply continued my cleaning.

And it all worked out fine.

I also want to confess that I remember thinking, just weeks earlier, that it seemed odd that I'm now 53 and I've never been in the hospital or had surgery.

I had also written a blog post that had the headline, "I No Longer Exist." (I've since changed it to "I Am Alive and Well.")

Well, my unconscious decided to deliver the experience to me.

By focusing on it, I began to attract it. I basically asked for it.

So, did I attract my emergency surgery?

As Rocky would say, "Absolutely."

The bottom line: You need to maintain constant vigilance over your mind. But since you can't yet be aware of what the larger operating system of your mind is doing, you must continue working to get clear.

But how?

# No Loopholes

*Criticism is never loving; it is never shared for someone's good. It is designed to undermine or create insecurities and doubt in the person to whom it is directed.*

—Karen Casey, *Change Your Mind and Your Life Will Follow*

I sometimes watch the ABC television show *Boston Legal*. In one 2007 episode, actor William Shatner, playing egomaniac attorney Denny Crain, sits in a chair, closes his eyes, and tries to attract actress Raquel Welch. He said he was going to attract world peace but thought a "smaller thing" like attracting a famous actress would be easier.

I loved seeing the movie *The Secret* and the Law of Attraction getting spoofed on national TV.

But that's what it was: a spoof.

At the end of the show Shatner's character attracts one of the greatest female comedians of all time: Phyllis Diller.

Shatner is shattered.

He thinks the Law of Attraction didn't work.

He mumbles, "I'm going to sue those people."

What did Shatner's character do wrong?

Why didn't he attract who he said he wanted?

Here's my take on it:

First, Shatner's character sits and concentrates, finger to forehead, and looks like he has a headache. There's no joy on his face. The Law of Attraction works when you *feel* the end result of what you want, not just think about it. Denny Crain isn't even close.

Second, Shatner's character takes no action at all. None. Considering the character he plays, surely he could have picked up the phone and called around. Surely someone in his power circle would be able to connect him to Raquel Welch. *I could get to her if I really wanted to.*

Third, Shatner's character attracts who he thinks he doesn't want: Phyllis Diller. This is *so* relevant. You always attract what you *unconsciously* think is right for you. In the TV show, Diller is actually an old flame. She represents sex to him, or at least did at one time. This is so Freudian. In order to get what you want, you have to get clear inside of the old programs. Until you do, you won't get what you *say* you want; you'll get what you *unconsciously* want.

Finally, Shatner's mumble at the end about suing those people is also revealing. It shows Shatner's character is still a victim, powerless in the world unless he resorts to the one thing he can manipulate: the legal system.

Again, I loved the episode on *Boston Legal.*

Just remember it was a spoof.

When it comes to the Law of Attraction there are no exceptions—not even for William Shatner.

But let's look a little deeper . . .

Besides Larry King interviewing me in November 2006 and again in March 2007, I'm being interviewed every day by other biggies, including *TIME* magazine, *Bottomline Personal,* and *Newsweek.* They all want to know if the Law of Attraction is really a law. They all agree that gravity is, but they aren't so sure about attraction.

The people who say attraction is not a law cite examples such as, "I know gravity works. When I drop a book off a skyscraper, it will hit the ground. That's proof of the law of gravity."

Agreed.

They then go on to say, "When I try to attract something, sometimes I get it and sometimes I don't. So it isn't a law."

Not agreed.

Here's why.

Saying you tried to attract something and failed is like saying you tried to drop a book from a skyscraper *to hit a particular spot* and you missed. Because you missed the spot, you say gravity doesn't exist.

This is a little like telling parachutists that because they didn't land on the red dot in the field, but instead landed in the trees, gravity doesn't exist.

Obviously gravity exists. You just don't know how to use it to get what you want in any specific way.

It's the same with the Law of Attraction.

When you focus on attracting a new car but instead attract a moped, it isn't because the law wasn't in effect; it's because you attracted exactly what you believed. In reality, you probably never expected to get a new car. Maybe you felt you didn't deserve it. Maybe you felt you could never afford it. Whatever you felt was what engaged the Law of Attraction.

Again, there are no exceptions to the Law of Attraction. As for the naysayers out there, William Walker Atkinson said it best when he wrote the following in *Thought Vibration*:

> Some time ago I was talking to a man about the Attractive Power of Thought. He said that he did not believe that Thought could attract anything to him, and that it was all a matter of luck. He had found, he said, that ill luck relentlessly

pursued him, and that everything he touched went wrong. It always had, and always would, and he had grown to expect it. When he undertook a new thing he knew beforehand that it would go wrong and that no good would come of it. Oh, no! There wasn't anything in the theory of Attractive Thought, so far as he could see; it was all a matter of luck!

This man failed to see that by his own confession he was giving a most convincing argument in favor of the Law of Attraction. He was testifying that he was always expecting things to go wrong, and that they always came about as he expected. He was a magnificent illustration of the Law of Attraction—but he didn't know it, and no argument seemed to make the matter clear to him. He was "up against it," and there was no way out of it—he always expected the ill luck— and every occurrence proved that he was right, and that the Mental Science position was all nonsense.

In short, everything you have is what you attracted. There are no loopholes to this law. There are no escape clauses. What you got, you attracted.

You just did it unconsciously.

No biggie.

No need to feel bad or beat yourself up.

Blame isn't as important as responsibility.

The idea now is to awaken.

How?

With The Key.

# Is Action Always Necessary?

*Success is the sum of small efforts, repeated day in and day out.*

—Robert Collier

When using the ideas in my book *The Attractor Factor*, or in the movie *The Secret*, you don't always need to take action. Sometimes—even often—what you want will come about almost without you doing anything. More often than not, though, you have to do *something*.

When Larry King's office called me on a Wednesday night to appear on his show a second time *the very next day*, my part was to rush to the Austin, Texas, airport and get to CNN in Los Angeles. I had to do a lot of sprinting to make it to the show. That's action. But the action I took was easy because it was part of the natural process of attracting another miracle.

My view of action is different from most people's. In my book *The Attractor Factor*, I call what you need to do "inspired action." If you get an inner prompt to make a call or buy a book or attend an event or apply for a job, then honor that nudge. Act on it.

That nudge is coming from the part of you connected to the greater picture. That part of you can lead you to the fulfillment of your goal. It will send the nudge, but you have to act on it.

My other point about action is that when you are clear about what you want and willing to do whatever it takes to achieve it, the action you take will be effort free.

I've written about this before. I write a tremendous number of books. For many, this would seem like work. For me, it is effort free. I'm certainly working, but the mind-set I have is that this is as natural as breathing.

Some say *The Secret* leads many to believe action isn't necessary. The fact is, I'm in the movie saying, "The universe likes speed. Don't delay. Don't second-guess. Don't doubt. When the opportunity is there, when the impulse is there, when the intuitive nudge from within is there, *act*. That's your job. That's all you have to do."

Action may or may not be necessary in your situation. It depends on you and what you want. More often than not, you'll have to take some sort of action. Part of the message of The Key is to pay attention to the signs and jump when it feels like it's part of the divine plan.

When you do, miracles happen.

Here's an example of what I mean:

When I was diagnosed with swollen lymph nodes in my chest and told they could be deadly, I stated an intention. I used what I didn't want (step one in *The Attractor Factor*), those swollen lymph nodes, to declare what I *did* want: to be completely free of any health problems. So I stated this intention: "I intend to erase and release the swollen lymph nodes so I am completely healthy."

Most people who state an intention leave it at that. They don't do anything else. Sometimes you don't have to do anything else. Sometimes your intention will trigger whatever is needed in you to heal the problem. But more often than not, you have to do something. It may be big or small, but usually there is action required on your part to attract the result you want.

In my case, I felt an inner prompt to write to a few friends who might be able to help me. Remember, I didn't have a logical reason to write these people. I may have rationalized that I wanted their emotional support, but what I was really doing was acting on an inspired nudge. I took action.

One of the people I wrote to was Joseph Sugarman, president of BluBlocker Corporation and author of numerous books, such as *Triggers*. To my surprise, Joe told me he had been working with a group of scientists overseas to create a supplement that actually cures cancer and dissolves tumors. While it wasn't on the market yet, he could get me a supply of it if I was interested. You can imagine my delight—and my interest. I instantly said I wanted information. Joe sent me a report that read, in part:

> The product is a new form of glutathione. If you aren't familiar with glutathione, you should be. Glutathione is a naturally produced antioxidant that has been cited in a massive amount of scientific literature. These studies confirm and support its disease-fighting abilities and immune-boosting properties. And I'm talking about 70,000 studies. But there is a problem.
>
> As we age, our body produces less glutathione. Much less. Our cells, which desperately need the additional glutathione, start to die because our body lacks the ability to produce enough to keep up with the daily damage our cells and bodies go through.
>
> And supplementation doesn't work that effectively. Either the synthetic glutathione is practically destroyed in the bloodstream when it is injected or it is destroyed in the stomach when it is swallowed. How do you capture the full antioxidant power of glutathione without destroying it before it gets to your cells? Enter the smelliest pill in the nation.

Protectus 120 is the world's first "protected" glutathione. In short, it is protected as it goes through the stomach and reaches the cells as a fat soluble substance. And since the cells are fat soluble, they easily absorb Protectus 120 right through the cell walls and provide the immune-boosting and repair functions that we only enjoyed in our youthful years.

I of course asked Joe to send me the product *right now*, even though it wasn't on the market yet and there wasn't a supply of it anywhere. (You can read about Protectus 120 today at www.stemcellproductsllc.com/protected-glutathione.htm.) Within minutes he put me in touch with the scientists who researched and created it. Within days I had the product on my doorstep. I began taking it that very moment.

None of this would have happened had I not taken action. But I didn't stop there.

I also reached out to healers I had known or heard about. Again, I felt inspired to contact them. One of them, Howard Wills, spent several phone sessions working on me with his energy healing. Another, Ann Taylor, spent an hour working on me by phone. Yet another, John Roper, said prayers over me. Kathy Bolden did several long-distance healing sessions for me. I also went to see Roopa and Deepak Chari at the Chari Center for Healing in San Diego. On top of all this, I also contacted medical doctors, such as Marc Gitterle, and a wellness consultant and chiropractor, Dr. Rick Barrett.

I took *a lot* of action. I admit that some of the action I took was based in fear. In other words, if I were more trusting about the power of intention, I might not have done so much. But I would have done *something*, and whatever it was would have been based on an inspired nudge. And yes, I believe it was as a result of the steps I took that those swollen lymph nodes became harmless.

When you implement The Key, be alert for nudges from within to do something. Do your best to ascertain if it is a nudge based in fear, or in love. If you want to resist the action, it is a sign you probably need to take it. As you use the steps to get clear in this book, you will take whatever action is needed to attract the result you want. It will happen naturally.

Finally, consider this: You don't always have to do everything or even anything to attract the result you want, but you do have to be *willing* to do whatever action surfaces for you. Your willingness to take action is a sign you are clear. When you are clear, you get the result you want (or something even better).

That's the promise of The Key.

# How to Attract a Million Dollars

*"I'm completely satisfied, I just want more!"*

—Britta Alexandra, aka Miss Bootzie

As I mentioned earlier, the universe (the Divine, God, or whatever it is for you) sends an idea into the mental world to several people at the same time. The Divine knows not all of those people will take action. In a way, it's just covering its bet.

But the person who takes action on the idea fastest is first to market, and usually profits the most. The first gets the biggest reward, and gets it first. The others can still act on the idea and still do well, but generally the first to come out of the gate with a new idea is the first to cash in big on it.

Here's an example of how this works:

One day a friend of mine called while I was busy. He left a message saying he had an idea for a million-dollar product. He left me a quick summary of the idea.

Now here's the punch line:

While he was *leaving* his message, I was out *creating* that very idea.

In other words, the universe sent the same idea to him, me, and most likely a few others. But when the idea entered my world, I acted on it. Fast. I was actually creating the idea while the others, including my friend, were still thinking about it.

I've said it before and I'll say it again: Money likes speed; the universe likes speed. When you get an idea, act.

The only reason you won't act quickly is due to hesitation of some sort. That hesitation is what needs to be cleared. That's what you need The Key for. When you get clear, you know what to do, and you just do it.

And consider this: My friend was not at all upset when he learned that I had already acted on the same idea he had received. He knew he could still produce his product. He also knew there's no scarcity in the world. He supported me and I supported him.

This is the kind of win-win you will experience all the time when you practice The Key.

Here's another example:

Last weekend my chiropractor, Dr. Rick Barrett of www.healedbymorning.com, saw me carrying a soft leather bag, something of a stylish saddlebag, and said he wanted one just like it. The thing is, I bought the bag over a year ago for $150 and didn't think I could get another one. The man who sold me the bag specialized in selling belt buckles and belts. His bags were a one-time offer. But I mentally told myself I would see if I could attract one for Dr. Barrett.

I would think about the bag every day, at least for a moment or two. I would tell myself that I want to find the man I bought it from and ask him about the bag. But I kept letting it go and doing other things.

But then yesterday I received an e-mail, out of the blue, from the very man who sold me the bag. He was checking to see if I had received a belt and belt buckle he had sent me as a gift. I thought it was amazing that he wrote me, as I hadn't heard from him in well over six months. But I seized the opportunity to reply and to of course ask about the leather bags.

He instantly wrote back, saying he doesn't sell the bags anymore. But he looked in storage and found two bags there, of different sizes. He offered to send them both to me, for free.

He said, "You are such an Attractor Factor guy that I feel like just giving these to you."

I was stunned.

But I also knew this is how the Law of Attraction works if you are clear inside: You state what you would like to have, but without any attachment to the outcome. You just playfully put it out there. When the universe puts the opportunity in your face, you take action. That's it.

And notice the win-win-win here:

Not only will Dr. Barrett get to choose the bag he wants from two different-size bags, but I'll get the other bag to use as I please.

And the man who is giving me the two bags?

I'm sending him a box of gifts, such as *The Missing Secret* DVD set, my *Humbug* DVD, my recent book *Buying Trances: A New Psychology of Sales and Marketing*, and a few other surprise goodies.

And he's also getting some publicity, as I'm giving you his name and web site: Rob McNaughton of www.robdiamond. net/.

This is how the Law of Attraction works: When you are clear inside, you get what you want or you get something even better than what you consciously want. But if you aren't clear inside, you often keep hitting blocks—and usually the same ones.

Last night the famous action-packed movie *Die Hard 2*, starring Bruce Willis, was on television. The lead character, who barely survived terrorists in the first movie, is again barely surviving bad guys in the second movie. At one point Bruce Willis says, "Why do these things keep happening to me?" I said out loud to the screen, "It's the Attractor Factor, bro."

Until he uses The Key to get clear, he'll keep attracting the same stuff, and never realize *he's* the magnet.

Not being clear makes for a great movie but a lousy life.

# Why Material Things?

*The forgiving state of mind is a magnetic power for attracting good.*

—Catherine Ponder

Sometimes readers wonder why the focus of people who read my books or watch the movie *The Secret* is on things like attracting a new car or new house or even happiness. Some regard those as "small, selfish things."

The truth is, so many people are unhappy, unhealthy, and just plain broke that using The Key to get a car, a house, a job, or happiness is simply the most noble thing they can do at the time. It's also exactly what they should do. It's not selfish so much as it is a step toward self-actualization.

People sometimes say the focus of people who use the Law of Attraction is too much on the material. What they don't understand is that the material and the spiritual are one. You are a physical being, but your essence is spirit. Everything you want is a symbol—an apparently concrete reality that is actually made up of energy. That energy is spirit. The material and the spiritual are two sides of the same coin. Wanting something material is a first step to awakening to the spirit within it, and you, and all things.

I know that at a certain point you set your sights higher. After you've manifested a car or two, or more money, or a better relationship, you start expanding your desires. You begin to realize that anything is possible. You begin to want to help others and even the planet. There are already numerous people in the world doing just that: using the

Law of Attraction to cure cancer, AIDS, poverty, and more.

Oprah is a good example. She openly admits to using the principle in *The Secret* and is doing historic work in third world countries. Larry King is another, with his cardiac foundation. Heavyweight boxing champion George Foreman is still another, with his youth centers.

Many of the teachers in *The Secret* have huge causes, too.

Jack Canfield wants to transform politics. Lisa Nichols is going to Africa to help people there. I'm working on erasing homelessness and poverty, both of which I've experienced. I'm also helping people (with the aid of fitness trainer Scott York) build their businesses as well as their bodies with www.your-businessbody.com.

Then there are the people you've never heard of, who are using the Law of Attraction to make a huge difference. Cynthia Mann created the Red Lipstick Campaign to raise money to help women with cancer get beauty treatments so they feel better about themselves. And there's Tammy Nerby, the female comedian who is raising audiotaped greetings and applause to send to troops overseas so they feel loved.

The list goes on.

Since the cultural mind-set with the bigger problems is one of being victims, those issues may not be healed overnight. But rest assured, there are wonderful people working on those problems and using ideas in *The Secret* and *The Attractor Factor* to get the job done.

On top of all those aspects is the idea that learning how to attract something material is how you prove to yourself that these ideas work. If you don't have a job but use The Key to get one, you just proved it works. If you don't have a car in your driveway but you then use the ideas in this book to attract one, the new car is hard evidence that you are learning how to create your own reality. That material then becomes a way to document your evolution in awakening.

But here's what's more important:

Instead of wondering what everyone else is doing, ask what *you* are doing.

How are *you* helping the world?

What causes are *you* creating or supporting?

How are *you* contributing to the betterment of the planet?

When you start thinking about what you want for yourself, also think about what you want for the world. We are in this adventure together. What you choose to attract could help the world, if you have that awareness. I am encouraging you to think more inclusively than you ever thought before, and to include noble causes when you do so. You don't have to be Mother Teresa, but you can be a quiet angel doing good deeds in your own world.

As Mahatma Gandhi said, "Be the change you want to see in the world."

Are you?

Will you?

When?

# Your Threshold of Deservingness

*Never look to society as a model of functional behavior and paradigms.*

—Dr. Bruce Goldberg, *Karmic Capitalism*

Most people complain that they don't have enough money.

They look at their bills, they look at their wants and needs, they look at their checkbook, and then they look terrified.

How will they pay their bills?

How will they feed their family?

How will they attract more money?

I'm sure you know the feeling. We've all been there. You may be there right now.

But what's *really* curious to me is this:

The movie *The Secret* and many of the teachers in it offer proven ways to attract money and other material things. This obviously works, given the thousands of testimonials from people who now have money when previously they couldn't find it in a bank with the vault door open.

But some people are complaining that the focus of the movie is only on money or material things. They say it's self-serving. They say it's egotistic.

Do you hear the cultural programming at work?

"Money is bad."

"Taking care of yourself is bad."

"Material things are not spiritual."

Please note the discrepancy: When you want money and at the same time say focusing on it is bad or selfish, *you are pushing it away.*

Even the *fans* of the movie are doing this. Some of the very people who use the Law of Attraction to get out of debt or acquire a new car attract only so much money before they begin to think they are being selfish. At that point they unconsciously turn off the flow and wonder what happened. They then begin to criticize the movie, too.

It's a strange thing to see.

First, people scramble to find money and worry and fret about it.

Then, they actually learn how to attract it, get some, and begin to complain that money isn't spiritual.

Wait a minute. Weren't these the same people who wanted money in the first place? Why was money good when they didn't have it and bad when they finally got it?

All of this is because of people's beliefs. They hit their threshold of deservingness.

My father plays the lottery. But when the lotto gets to a hundred million dollars, he quits playing. He says that amount is "too much" and "*that* much money will ruin you."

Again, we're dealing with beliefs. We're dealing with thresholds of deservingness.

I was at an event once when a fellow called his wife and handed me the phone. He wanted a star of The Secret to surprise her. I took the call, said my name, and heard her scream. She was talking to a celebrity. She was giddy with excitement. But then she started asking me what I was doing to save the world.

This woman had gone from being a fan of The Secret and using what she learned to manifest a few things to being critical now that she had hit her comfort zone and did not want anything else.

What happened?

I write a blog at www.blog.mrfire.com. I sometimes write about one of my favorite cars, named Francine. She's a 2005 Panoz Esperante GTLM, a hand-assembled exotic luxury sports car. I love Francine. But not everyone loves me writing about her. One person who reads my blog regularly wrote the following:

> I used to get upset when you wrote about all your cars, but now I see you were simply pushing my button. The button is inside me. It had nothing to do with you or your cars. I wasn't okay with wealth, and so I didn't like to see it flaunted by others. Now I enjoy hearing you talk about Francine. Thank you for helping to dissolve my inner limits.

That reader recognized his threshold of deservingness. Once he was aware of it, he was able to easily raise it to a new level.

Another example is this: Many of the teachers in the movie *The Secret* create products and services to help you achieve your goals. When your mind-set is open, you thank them for their services. When your mind-set is closed, you say they are just "selling."

Well, are they selling or serving?

It's both and it's neither. It depends on your beliefs. It depends on your threshold of deservingness. If you think they are taking advantage of you, you call it selling (because you think selling is bad). If you think they are helping you, you call it serving (because you know serving is good).

Again, it's all about beliefs, and particularly your belief about what you feel you *deserve*. *That* belief creates a threshold that you won't get past without some work using clearing methods like those in this book.

It reminds me of a question a therapist used to ask patients:

"How good can you stand it?"

Most of us can't stand it *really* good.

"What will the neighbors think?"

"What will my family think?"

"If it's *too* good, surely something bad will happen."

"I don't deserve to have things too good."

"If it's too good, it won't last and I'll be miserable again."

"If I'm happy, I won't do anything to save the planet."

Those are all limiting beliefs.

Your life can be fantastic. Truly amazing. But very often we hit a comfort level and won't go past it. Why? Because of our self-imposed limits. Because of our threshold of deserving-ness.

You can deceive yourself with rationalizations and criticisms about *The Secret*, me, others, the world, and so on; but the end result is that *you* limit your own good.

I keep reminding people that once you get clear using The Key, there's not much you can't have, do, or be. In fact, I doubt there are any limits at all. The only limits we have are based on our current understanding of reality, and that keeps changing as we keep raising the bar on what's possible. Your goal should always be happiness, what I call spiritual awakening, but the only limits along the way are your own.

How good *can* you stand it, anyway?

# Expect Miracles

*The thing always happens that you really believe in; and the belief in a thing makes it happen.*

—Frank Lloyd Wright

This book reveals and explains 10 proven ways to get clear and awaken so you can consciously engage the Law of Attraction. Each method is designed to be completed by yourself, so you don't need any more books, teachers, or anything else. There's nothing wrong with more books or teachers, but I've designed this book to be a stand-alone tool. I want it to be your one-stop place for personal transformation.

You can read this book however you feel directed to do so. I suggest you read it front to back first, just like you would a novel, to get a sense of what's here. You can then jump to whatever technique seems to pull you. Trust yourself. Enjoy the process. My rule of thumb is to do what's fun. If you have to do something that doesn't seem like fun, find a way to change your perspective of it or get someone else (who thinks it's fun) to do it. When it comes to personal growth work, you can't delegate. But you *can* choose whatever method appeals the most to you at any given time. You have choice.

Before you jump any further into The Key, let me also remind you that if you do want support in this adventure into a life of magic and miracles, consider the Miracles Coaching program (it's described at www.miraclescoaching.com). Again, this book is designed to be all you need, but as you'll discover as you read on, sometimes support can accelerate the process of change. (In fact, in Alan Deutschman's book *Change or Die*, the first step to creating lasting change is to have a support team.)

Before you begin the methods in this book, write down some things you'd like to be, do, or have. This is important. When you state your intention, you align your thoughts to begin to work toward it. You engage the Law of Attraction.

But something magical also happens. You also place an order with the universe (whatever you call that power that is greater than all of us), and it will begin to bring what you want to you, and put you in situations that will help you attract what you want. It will also bring up anything in the way of you attracting what you want, so you have the opportunity to clear obstacles.

This isn't magic, though it will often feel like it. Instead, it's using the natural laws of the universe to align yourself with the experience you want to attract.

Remember to think big. As I wrote in an earlier book, *Life's Missing Instruction Manual*, my favorite motto is the sixteenth-century Latin phrase *Aude aliquid dignum*, which means "Dare something worthy."

Well, if you could have anything—dare anything—what would it be?

And while you're thinking, consider this: In my book *The Greatest Money-Making Secret in History*, I suggested you "think like God." What does that mean? If you had powers to do, be, or have anything, what would you do? Remember, God has no limits. If you thought like God, would you worry about anything? Would you worry about excuses? The idea is to *pretend* you are God as you contemplate the life you wish to attract.

With those thoughts in mind, what do you want?

Write it down here or in a journal:

_____

_____

_____

_____

_____

_____

_____

_____

_____

_____

_____

_____

_____

_____

_____

_____

_____

_____

_____

_____

_____

_____

*The way we choose to see the world creates the world we see.*

—Barry Neil Kaufman

# Think Bigger!

*If you don't know you can't, you can. If you don't know you can, you can't.*

—Gene Landrum, *The Superman Syndrome*

Now let me nudge you a little. Look over your list of goals and desires and ask yourself if you've been honest. In other words, what do you *really* want that you didn't put on the list, maybe because you thought it was impossible or you didn't know how to achieve it?

The idea here is to think bigger than you've ever thought before. And think of others, as well. Often intentions are more powerful when they include helping others. In other words, wanting more money for yourself is good, but wanting more money for you and your family is even better.

According to Peter Ressler and Monika Mitchell Ressler in their book, *Spiritual Capitalism*, Albert Einstein said, "A human being experiences himself, his thoughts and feelings, as something separated from the rest—a kind of optical illusion of his consciousness. This illusion is a prison for us, restricting us to our personal desires and to affection for only the few people nearest us. Our task must be to free ourselves from the prison by widening our circle of compassion to embrace all living beings and all of nature."

There's nothing wrong with huge, worthy ideals like wanting peace on earth, feeding the starving, or housing the homeless. These may seem impossible at first glance. But I believe in miracles. I believe anything is possible—no exceptions. You may not know how to achieve something, and maybe no one has ever done it before, but that doesn't mean it can't happen. You may be the one to cure or solve—you name it.

So in the space that follows write your ruthlessly honest goals. Again, don't concern yourself with how you'll achieve something. Once you state your intention, you'll begin to think of possibilities for attracting it. After you complete the different clearing exercises in this book, you'll be well on your way to attracting miracles.

Write down your biggest intentions here or in your journal:

_____

_____

_____

_____

_____

_____

_____

_____

_____

_____

_____

_____

_____

_____

_____

_____

_____

Happy reading and *expect miracles!*

# Part Two

# The Methods

*This concept of the universe as a world of pure thought throws a new light on many situations we have encountered in our survey of modern physics.*

—Sir James Jeans, physicist, mathematician, astronomer

# Clearing Method #1

## You Are Here

*Happiness depends more on the inward disposition of mind than on outward circumstances.*

—Benjamin Franklin

One day I drove into Austin, Texas, and met with the staff that runs my Miracles Coaching program and my Executive Mentoring program. I had some exciting news to share with them, and some astonishing news arrived while I was there.

In the morning the *Today* show called, wanting information on my then forthcoming book, *Zero Limits*. That's pretty big, but not as big as the news that came later.

At lunch I handed out the recently completed bibliography of my life's work so far—45 pages of books, e-books, audios, videos, software, fitness formulas, and more—an entire listing of everything I've created up to now. The heft of the document alone impressed even me.

But that wasn't the biggest news of the day, either.

At lunch with the staff, I stood up and told them something that I felt inspired to share. I put a dot on the whiteboard on the wall and circled it.

"You are here," I said.

I told them the whiteboard was like the map at the mall where all the stores are listed and a little box says "You are here" to give you your bearings.

"Where do you want to go from here?" I asked.

"Up," someone said.

"Up off the whiteboard itself," someone else said.

"This is all good," I went on. "You all want to move up. You want more sales, more results, and more wealth. Right?"

They all agreed.

I then put another dot on the board, way up at the top of it, and circled it.

"That represents where you want to go," I said.

I then asked the key question: "How do you go from where you are to where you want to be?"

They were quiet for a moment, but then began saying things like "Take a straight line," and "Do one thing at a time," and "Make more sales calls," and so on.

"That's all good," I said. "Those are all practical answers. But I want you to think in terms of the movie, *The Secret* and my book, *The Attractor Factor*."

I added, "I'm going to tell you what I think is the greatest secret to manifesting whatever you want."

They were quiet, not sure where I was going with all this.

"Does anyone want to know what the secret is?" I asked.

They all burst out laughing. They definitely wanted to know.

I pointed at the first "You are here" dot and said, "The secret to getting what you want is to totally appreciate this moment. When you are grateful for this moment, then whatever is next for you will bubble up out of this moment. You'll be inspired to take action of some sort. That will lead you up. But the only way to get to the upper dot is to live in this dot with gratitude."

They'd all heard this before, but I wanted them to truly get it.

I then told them about my Maui friend, Bootzie, who says my favorite line these days: "I'm totally satisfied, I just want more."

That's the key to success, I explained.

It's wanting more without needing more.

I went on and on about being grateful, and how it leads to that upward climb. Most of us aren't happy right now, thinking we will be happy when we get to that other dot. But the great joke is that when you get to the other dot, you won't be happy. You'll be looking for another dot on the map. You'll use unhappiness to whip yourself forward. The thing is, it doesn't have to be that way.

Just be happy now.

Out of this now will come the miracles you seek.

The group got the message. They shook my hand. Smiled. Showed light in their eyes. Walked away with a spring in their step.

Now here's the really juicy part.

I got a phone call right after that meeting. It was Suzanne, my assistant. She almost never calls me, and she knew I was in a meeting. So I knew this call had to be important.

I took the call and to my delight I learned that Oprah's people wanted my media kit.

And they wanted it by midnight.

Oprah's folks are considering me as a guest for a show.

Oprah!

Now get this: I was happy in the moment. As I'm happy, the next moment brings its own rewards. As I'm happy in that moment, it, too, gives birth to more joy.

You can do this, too. You may not have Oprah call you, but you will get what is right for you. I explain all of this in the book *Zero Limits*. But the essence of the message is this:

All you have to do is embrace the dot that says, "You are here" and do what it tells you to do.

And when the phone rings, answer it!

This step is all about being grateful. I can't stress how important this one method can be in clearing you so you can have the
miracles you seek.

One day Robert Ringer interviewed me for his teleseminar.
He's the best-selling author of numerous books, such as
*Winning Through Intimation* and *Looking Out for #1*. He agreed
that gratitude was the ticket to success.

I explained that if you can begin feeling grateful for anything, even a pencil or this book or your socks, you can change
your inner state. When you do, you begin to attract more to be
grateful for.

When I was on the *Larry King Live* show the first time, my
friend Jack Canfield, coauthor of the *Chicken Soup for the Soul*
series of books and of *The Success Principles*, said that author
John DeMartini does not get out of bed in the morning
until a tear of gratitude rolls down his face. You can imagine
how wonderful he feels when he begins his day with that
exquisite feeling.

I spent part of yesterday in San Antonio with a dear friend.
We talked at length about life and spirituality. I told him
that most people are not in the moment. They are looking
for the next deal, next car, next house, next pay raise, next
check—not realizing that the point of power, the true
miracle, is right here.

The quest for the "stuff" is a grand illusion. There's nothing
wrong with any of it, as long as you know it's part of the game

of life. But most people think it will bring lasting happiness. It won't. As soon as you achieve it or attract it, you'll desire something else. You'll be chasing the next moment. The trick is to be in this moment while playfully wanting more. No need. No attachment. No addiction. Just gratiude for now while welcoming even more.

I told my friend about the Adam Sandler movie *Click*. The essence of the movie is that Adam is trying to fast-forward through life. He does, too. But near the end of his life he realizes he missed out on life itself.

I do my best not to leave the moment. I still do, of course. I'm learning, too. But I do my best to stay here, in this moment, knowing that as I do, the next moment takes care of itself. As long as I fully participate in this moment, the next ones are just as good and often incredibly better.

In fact, when you stay in the moment, you attract more of the good things in life and appreciate them longer. The key is to be here now, with awareness and gratitude.

This clearing method is all about being here now with gratitude. When you are, you begin to attract even more to be grateful for. This is a powerful secret for using The Key to attract more of what you prefer. It all begins with gratitude.

I fully realize you may be thinking that you have too many bills, or too much pain, or too much worry to feel grateful for anything at all. But there's always *something* to be grateful for. Always. It's a matter of choosing to see it. You might be grateful for this book. The roof over your head. Your friends. Your chair. Your life. Start wherever you can, because feeling grateful is the fastest way to attract a miracle.

In fact, feeling grateful lets you know the miracle is already happening, right now. As Socrates said, "He who is not

contented with what he has would not be contented with
what he would like to have."

Maybe this story will help you feel grateful right now:

About three years ago Kevin Hogan, author of *The Science of
Influence* and many other books, told me about a little boy he
met named Kirk. The child had suffered a pediatric stroke a
few weeks after birth. Apparently this can happen to babies,
more often than anyone likes to know.

Kevin asked me to help him raise money for medical
care and operations, and I did. As a result, Kirk is moving
a little, and smiling a lot. Kirk sends me little "I love you"
messages and photos—by e-mail via his mother—and every
one of them makes me smile. I received one the other day and
stared at it for minutes, looking at Kirk's contagiously happy
smile, and feeling drawn into the loving spirit of this child.

It feels good to help someone of such a divine nature, who
seems happy to be where he is in life—no complaints, no
bickering, no bitterness.

Who knows why someone like Kirk comes into the world
and instantly has a health challenge? Is it karma? Reincarna-
tion? Or—?

Maybe it's a divine test for us—not Kirk, as he is Buddha
happy right now—but a test for *you and me*; it's *us* who seem to
be challenged by his situation. *We* are the ones being asked to
grow here, not Kirk.

The truth is, I don't know the why. But I do know that when
something is in my experience, I attracted it and it's up for me
to heal. So I'm doing my part. I'm helping Kirk with donations
to his therapy fund, and with talking about him on my blog

and in my books, like right now (Kirk's web site is www.ama-
zingkirk.com).

Consider Kirk's life and ask yourself what *you* have to
complain about. Start smiling, too. You have much to be
grateful for, don't you?

In this section I invite you to experience this magical clearing
technique. In the space that follows, or in a journal of your
own, write out what you are grateful for. It can be a list, an
experience, or anything you can imagine or recall.

_____

_____

_____

_____

_____

_____

_____

_____

_____

_____

_____

_____

_____

_____

_____

_____

# Clearing Method #2
## Opting to Change Inner Beliefs

*Although it may not seem obvious at first, people are actually unhappy because they want or choose to be.*

—Bruce Di Marsico

You live in a belief-driven universe. What you believe is what you get. But if that's so, how do you change your beliefs so you change your results?

One of the most powerful tools I have ever come across for getting clear is a simple questioning process called Option. It was created by Bruce Di Marsico and popularized by Barry Neil Kaufman, author of *To Love Is to Be Happy With*. I never met Bruce but I did study with Barry. I also studied with other students of Bruce's, including Mandy Evans, author of *Travelling Free*.

Mandy and I have worked together for more than 30 years. Whenever I feel "unclear," I book an Option session with her. She has helped me release limiting beliefs about money, about health, and about relationships. When my wife died, I called Mandy. When I wanted my income to soar, I called Mandy. When I wanted to lose weight, I called Mandy.

While Mandy is wonderful, the tool she uses to help me and others is the real gift. It's a simple questioning process, based on love. It's designed to explore why we are unhappy.

Whenever you don't get what you want, there is an accompanying emotion. Call it anger, frustration, grief, depression, sadness, rage, or anything else; they are all variations of the word *unhappiness*.

What Mandy does is help you explore your reasons for feeling the way you do. As you explore, you release. As you release, you are free. From there, miracles are possible.

I asked Mandy to explain her method for you. Here's what she wrote.

### How to Use the Option Method Dialogue to Question Unhappiness

#### By Mandy Evans
© 2007

You can improve anything in your life, from your relationships to your finances, when you discover the hidden beliefs that hold you back. Once you know what they are, you can question them to see if they are still true for you in the clear light of day.

You can liberate yourself from painful emotions like crippling fear, anger, or guilt by finding and dismantling the beliefs that cause them and keep them in place.

Instead of struggling in frustration to change circumstances and situations, you can change the beliefs that keep you stuck.

A limiting or self-defeating belief is one that causes unhappiness or keeps you from knowing and following your heart's desire. They color and shape every goal you reach for, even what dreams you dare to have. The beliefs that block happiness are among most limiting and self-defeating of all.

When you are happy and clear, though, you make choices and take actions that lead down a very different path from one you take in anger or fear. You arrive at a different place after an amazingly dissimilar trip.

I use the Option Method to help people to find and dismantle the beliefs they hold that block happiness, creativity, and success. One key element of this method is a question-and-answer Option Dialogue—sort of a belief interview with yourself.

To begin, accept yourself just as you are. If you judge yourself while you delve into your feelings and beliefs, you will not be able to see clearly or tell yourself the truth. Take your time. Learn as much about your feelings and beliefs as you can. Each question follows the answer to the one before it.

It helps to write your answers down. If you keep a journal, you can track your progress.

You have to be willing to go through some confusion. As your beliefs change, your version of reality breaks up and reforms—disorienting, to say the least! These questions and answers weave around sometimes. They make more sense when you ask them about *your* feelings and *your* beliefs.

Here are six basic Option Method questions you can ask to get clear:

1. *What are you unhappy about?* Or angry, guilty, worried, for example. This question helps you get specific about your feeling and what it is about.

2. *Why are you unhappy about that?* Our reasons for feeling bad are different from what we feel bad about. Our reasons are beliefs.

3. *What are you concerned would happen if you were not unhappy about that?* This odd-sounding question helps you find any fear or concern you have about the feeling going away. We are often reluctant to part with a feeling even if it is painful.

4. *Do you believe that?*

5. *Why do you believe that?*

6. *What are you concerned would happen if you did not believe that?* Sometimes we hold on to a long-held belief even if it

(continued)

proves limiting or causes unhappiness. What are your concerns? Do they still seem real to you?

Here is an example of an Option Dialogue I did with myself. It took only three questions to change my feelings and my life. I already knew I felt awful about the starving people in the world. I began with the second question.

*Why do you feel awful about that?*

*Answer:* Nobody seems to care. It is so unnecessary.

*What are you concerned would happen if you didn't feel awful?*

*Answer:* I wouldn't do anything about it.

*Do you believe that?*

*Answer:* No! As soon as I asked the question, I knew the worse I felt, the less I did. In fact when I felt really bad, I didn't want to think about it at all, much less do anything.

I felt better immediately. Now I take much more action, contribute more money, and look for ways to make a difference.

If someone asked me to review everything I learned in my whole life and give just one piece of helpful advice, it would be this—always question unhappiness. Never take feeling bad for granted.

Happiness is the grand prize in the game of life, and you can award it to yourself!

To your happiness!

Mandy Evans

www.mandyevans.com

I invite you to use Mandy's process on an emotion you may be feeling right now. Think of something you want to be, do, or have. If you haven't attracted it yet, how do you feel about it? Take that emotion and work with it here:

1. *What are you unhappy about?* Or angry, guilty, worried, for example. This question helps you get specific about your feeling and what it is about.

   _____

   _____

   _____

   _____

   _____

2. *Why are you unhappy about that?* Our reasons for feeling bad are different from what we feel bad about. Our reasons are beliefs.

   _____

   _____

   _____

3. *What are you concerned would happen if you were not unhappy about that?* This odd-sounding question helps you find any fear or concern you have about the feeling going away. We are often reluctant to part with a feeling even if it is painful.

   _____

   _____

   _____

   _____

   _____

   _____

   _____

4. *Do you believe that?*

   _____

   _____

   _____

5. *Why do you believe that?*

   _____

   _____

   _____

_____

_____

_____

_____

_____

_____

6. *What are you concerned would happen if you did not believe that?*
   Sometimes we hold on to a long-held belief even if it
   proves limiting or causes unhappiness. What are your
   concerns? Do they still seem real to you?

_____

_____

_____

_____

_____

_____

_____

_____

_____

_____

   At this point you should feel much clearer about the issue.
If something is still there, or a new emotion surfaces, simply
walk through the process again. The Option Method is a very
liberating and easy way to release stuck energy and limiting
beliefs. When you are free, you engage The Key to attract
whatever you want.

# Clearing Method #3
## Unraveling Your Thoughts

*If we all worked on the assumption that what is accepted as true were really true, there would be little hope of advance.*

—Orville Wright

The Key is all about getting clear of the hidden thoughts or beliefs that are attracting what you don't want. In other words, you might say you want to attract a mate, but you keep attracting poor matches. You might say you want to attract the perfect home, but you keep moving into dumps. You might say you want the perfect job, but you keep attracting ones you don't feel appreciated in.

Actually, you are attracting exactly what you think you deserve and expect. The point is to change that hidden mental wiring so you attract more of what you prefer.

I've found that by using belief-finding tools you can unearth the apparently hidden beliefs operating in your life. The beliefs are unconscious, but you can bring them to the surface with the right method. Another powerful and proven tool to help you unravel your own thoughts is in the field of cognitive psychology.

I've asked Dr. Larina Kase to help me explain and demonstrate how this works. Larina and I are coauthors of the e-book *How to End Self-Sabotage for Aspiring E-Book Authors* (www.endselfsabotage.com). Here's her original article, written just for you.

# Five Steps to Getting Clear with Cognitive Therapy

### By Dr. Larina Kase

Cognitive therapy (CT), pioneered by Dr. Aaron Beck, has four decades of research support and is a powerful way to clear any of your limiting beliefs. The key components of CT are your thoughts, feelings, behaviors, and biological responses. These characteristics all interact to determine your mood and actions. I'll share five simple steps to using CT to get clear.

First, identify your intrusive, upsetting, or disruptive thoughts. Write them down. This process is like catching butterflies with a net. Thoughts are quick and fleeting, and we are typically not even aware of them. When you identify your thoughts, you increase your awareness and can then work on changing the thoughts. If you find it difficult to catch your thoughts, pay close attention to shifts in your mood. As soon as you notice a change in your mood, ask yourself, "What just went through my mind?" You'll identify a powerful thought to work with.

Second, approach your thoughts like an impartial jury would evaluate evidence. Instead of assuming that your thoughts are true, gather evidence to assess their validity. Take a sheet of paper and divide it into three columns. In the first column, write the header "Emotional thought." In the second column write the column header "Evidence this thought is true," and in the third column write the header "Evidence this thought is not true." Fill in the columns with evidence for and against your emotional thought. This is like examining the butterfly with curiosity and without judgment.

Third, conduct some behavioral experiments to further test out the truth of the thought. If, for example, your thought was,

"I always say something stupid when speaking before a group," test out how true this really is by speaking in front of a lot of groups. Is it true that you always said something stupid? This step also helps you gain practice with the things you fear so they become easier over time and your confidence increases when your feared outcome doesn't occur.

Fourth, decide how true your original thought is based on the evidence you gathered and the results of your behavioral experiments. Consider how likely your fear is to occur. You'll probably realize that your upsetting thought is unlikely to come true. If there is a possibility of it coming true, ask yourself how you'd handle it. You'll see that you're resourceful and you could handle the challenging situation if it actually occurred.

Fifth, and finally, realize that your troubling or limiting thoughts are not necessary. They aren't helping you. Thoughts don't hurt you, either, so don't resist them. Remember that the more unwilling you are to experience something, the more likely you are to experience it. If you try to suppress a thought, it'll keep coming back like a song that gets stuck in your head. Don't hold on to your upsetting thoughts, but don't push them away, either. If they return in the future, simply let them drift away on their own. Let the butterflies go. You are now clear.

In the space that follows, or in your journal, use Larina's method to help you with a particular issue:

_____

_____

_____

_____

_____

_____

_____

## Clearing Method #4

### Hypnotic Stories

*There is something that you know but you don't know you know it.
As soon as you find out what it is that you already know, but you
don't know, you know then you can begin.*

—Milton H. Erickson

One of the most powerful clearing tools around is as simple as
what you are doing right now: reading.

Reading books that expand your mind can help you release
limiting beliefs. Whether you read Rhonda Byrne's *The Secret*,
Claude Bristol's classic *The Magic of Believing*, Debbie Ford's *The
Dark Side of the Light Chasers*, Jerry and Esther Hicks' *The Law of
Attraction*, Jack Canfield's *The Success Principles*, or even books like
my own *Zero Limits* or *The Attractor Factor*, all can help you realize
that a different reality is possible for you.

Part of the reason these books help you get clear is due to
the information in them. They educate you to believe in
miracles. But the books also work on your unconscious mind,
delivering a message of hope and new possibilities.

At heart, this is what I call hypnotic storytelling. I've
written about this in other books, such as *Hypnotic Writing*
and *Buying Trances*. Since I am a hypnotherapist, I know the
value of a good story to enter your mind and change your
beliefs. This happens easily and effortlessly. All you do is relax
and read.

One of the most skilled hypnotists on the planet is Mark
Ryan. He and I created a series of DVDs packed with stories
that change you from within as you watch the movies (you can

read about them at www.subliminalmanifestation.com).
I asked Mark to write a hypnotic story just for you. Again,
all you have to do is read it. You don't have to think. You don't
have to make notes. You don't have to do anything but read
the following.

## The Super Secret to Getting Clear

### By Mark J. Ryan

Secret: Start from your current level of belief.

I have had many cars in my life, most of which were used. I
noticed that over many years of buying cars, I would inevitably
have problems with them. I'd fix the problems, drive the car
for as long as possible, sell it for what I could get, and then buy
another.

I could tell when a major repair was coming and it was
therefore time to sell, as I used to repair cars years ago. I had
one car that had a lot of miles on it and I was getting ready to
let it go within a few months. It started to break down like
crazy, almost as if the car knew I was going to sell it. I really
didn't want to fix the problems, and I considered selling it even
cheaper than I had planned. But one day, I heard that still
small voice that told me I needed to fix the problems for the
next buyer instead of handing my problems over to that
person.

Would I invest in changing the dynamics of flow in the
universe? How much would that be worth?

I knew I would lose money on the deal at that point. It
would be a loss to me financially, but in another way, it was an
investment in relating to my fellow human beings and to the
universe.

I decided to get the universal reversal package . . . and invest.

I ended up spending about $1,000 on repairs and new tires for a car I was selling for about $1,000. When the guy came to buy that car, the gas tank had sprung a leak, and a pretty good leak at that.

I pointed the leak out to him and told him I'd fix it. He wanted the car right away, so I reduced the price to $750. The buyer was very happy with the deal, especially after seeing the receipts for the recent repairs I had made.

Remember this story as I tell you another one. I discovered a huge way to get clear by listening to this still, small voice within me, much like I did with the sale of that car.

For about 14 years, I had been living in a house that had been in my family for over 100 years.

And I wanted out.

I loved the house for all of the wonderful memories it had given me when my Grandma lived there. But the house had structural issues and lots of little things that needed fixing. All of these problems were things I didn't want to contend with.

I started doing some heavy manifestation work to move myself to California. I wanted to get away from the long winters in upstate New York and away from those house problems. I went to California many times for business and on vacations, but I never seemed to get myself moved there.

One day, I was lying in bed upstairs and feeling the heavy weight of those problems, and that still, small voice asked me what I would do to the house if I ended up staying there for a longer period of time. Not necessarily just making the house right for the next person who would live there, but what would I do to improve the environment for the person living in it right now—*me*!

I wrestled with that thought for a while. I didn't even want to think about it for fear I might get so excited about those

(*continued*)

improvements that I might manifest staying in a place where I didn't want to be any longer.

It seemed like a paradox, and yet I knew that if I ever wanted my dream home in California, then I needed to get to know what it felt like to be present, to like what I had in the present, and to know what it would take to make me happy there. I needed to be happy in the here and now, in my present circumstances, in my present house.

So many of us manifest from a place of thinking about what we *don't* want. We ask for something to be removed; we ask for something to get us away from our current problems, because we are looking for an escape.

Of course, the universe knows that this isn't what we truly want. It knows we are manifesting an escape from something, not manifesting the creation of something new. We're not manifesting from a present state of being completely clear.

The thought of escape only creates a new situation from which we'll also want an escape.

The thought of being in a place I love, in a place with which I am completely satisfied in the present, brings me more places I love from the present. And that in turn creates a new reality with even more of those qualities.

So, on a long, lined, yellow piece of paper, I wrote a list of seven things that would make me feel at peace in the current house and actually like the house again. (Who knows, maybe the house was influencing me to give it the things it wanted before it would let me go.)

I felt something in me open once I started writing that list, something very light and bright, and I could actually feel the emotions of enjoying the house I was in. What was closed and hard and made me feel like escaping was now opening. My mind opened along with my chest to a new feeling of loving that house in the present moment.

The more I focused on that feeling, the more I felt the opening. Ideas were coming to me about things that I couldn't figure out how to fix, like the back roof.

These small things to fix the problems where I was, not the big goal of the dream home in California, were leading me to the larger goal.

I found that long, lined, yellow piece of paper about a year later. I wondered what I had written on it. I then noticed that for the first time ever in writing my goals and intentions, every one of the seven things had been completed. The amazing thing was that it seemed that those things were completed effortlessly. Whenever I needed help completing a project, the right person would appear to help me with the job.

The front porch needed scraping and painting. One day, a delivery guy said, "Ryan, when are you going to paint your porch?" I replied, "When I find someone to do it." He offered to do it for $50 if I bought the paint. One job done! And while he was there, he also painted my garage and shed for another $250—a huge bargain!

Another day, a friend came by and noticed that my roof needed to be reshingled, another item on my list. He made me an offer. It was more than I had, but a relative offered me a loan, so I started the project.

While taking off the shingles, he discovered the real damage to the back of my house: Termites had destroyed the rafters and water had come in, creating black mold. We had to act fast and tear down and rebuild the back of my house.

Again, it was more money I didn't have. But for the price he offered, which was half of what anyone else would have charged, I knew it was going to happen.

As he described how he was going to fix it, he said he had an image in his mind to make the area even better than it was

(continued)

before. I listened in amazement as he described—almost word for word—the picture I had in my *own* mind almost a year before. I knew exactly why he was there.

He actually told me he felt as if he had been sent there to help me. And he did so much more freely because he felt like he was making up for his past as he cleaned up his future. He knew helping me would benefit him.

The removal of the hidden black mold from the back of my home had additional benefits. After two years of almost constant illness, I started feeling better. The universe knew and provided healing once I began to take action.

As I read the list from that yellow paper, I knew the secret. I knew what I had done differently than before.

The house looks and feels different. My neighbors compliment me on the improvement.

A good friend of mine might be moving to Hollywood to star in his own TV show. He asked if I would be interested in moving there if he went to Los Angeles. You can guess what I said.

My girlfriend wants to move to a sunny place. She has an agreement with the father of her child that they would choose a place together so that they both would be involved in their son's upbringing. They had been disagreeing for months on where that place would be. Every place on her list was met with resistance from him. Just yesterday, he was talking with her about moving to California. When she asked where, he said he had a strange pull to move south of San Francisco—in exactly the area that I have been wanting to move to. She never told him of our discussions and found it amazing that he felt a draw to the same area I had told her about.

California is calling!

So here's the Secret: Everything to get you clear exists within your reality right now!

What would it take to make you happy right here and now, right where you are sitting? Let your imagination run wild.

Here is the big distinction. Attach it to what already exists in your reality. What can you do to make your reality, here and now, as good as it can be? What can you do to improve your reality for the next person to come into that environment, whether it be a car, your home, your daily job, or your place in line at the bank? And more important, what can you do to make it better *for yourself*?

One last thought: When you let go of your California dream to clean up your here-and-now reality, *remember that the universe truly knows what you want*. When I let go of my California dream to focus on creating a better reality in my present world, I got much clearer on what I wanted in California, and on how I really wanted to *feel* when I was there.

Instead of creating my California dream as an escape, I created love in my present reality. And by creating love—and *giving* that love in my present reality—I am now creating a reality that will beget even more love. The real dream does not exist without the engine of love.

Instead of dumping a problem car on an unsuspecting buyer, I fixed those problems and created a car that I would feel good about selling to another person. By giving that car improvements from a place of love, I created an opening for a car that I will love to manifest in my life.

Create your engine of love in your present reality. Get very clear about how to express that love in the right way for you. Then, your highest dream will take care of the *how* of getting you to be the main character in that dream come true.

Mark Ryan's story is powerful. While you let it sit in your unconscious, let me tell you a brief story of my own:

Mark came to visit me for a few days in April 2007. We have fun conversations that are free to roam from subject to subject. We both enjoy whatever we discover as we share our stories, often over a cigar or a scotch whiskey.

One day Mark and I were going to visit friends. Neither of us was sure of the directions. Mark laughed and asked, "Did you ever see that episode of *Star Trek: The Next Generation*, when Jean-Luc Picard is asked where to go when they are lost on a new planet?"

"No," I said. "But I love those shows. Remind me."

"Jean-Luc declares that they are to come up to the mountain and turn left."

"Yeah?"

"Well, the woman with him can read his mind, and she says, 'You don't have a clue where we are, do you?'"

I laughed as Mark continued.

"Jean-Luc says he is the captain and has to appear confident, even when he isn't."

I loved that story. For the rest of the day I would make swift, confident decisions, even when I had no idea what was next or what I was doing. This role-playing made my day much more interesting and me much more powerful.

When Mark got a call from our friends asking when we would meet them, I told Mark, "We'll meet them at 6:23 PM."

I had no idea when we would meet them. But by acting as if I did, I had greater control over my experience. In fact, my life became a grand adventure with me as the captain of my ship.

And yes, we met with our friends—far earlier than expected. We found our way. Traffic opened up. And we arrived before they expected us to—pretty close to 6:23 PM.

# *Clearing Method #5*

## I Love You

*We are the sum total of our experiences, which is to say that we are burdened by our pasts. When we experience stress or fear in our lives, if we would look carefully, we would find that the cause is actually a memory.*

—Morrnah Simeona

Three years ago I heard about a Hawaiian therapist who helped heal an entire ward of mentally ill criminals—without seeing any of them in his office. I later met him, studied with him, and coauthored a book with him, called *Zero Limits*. His method is a powerful tool for sweeping out all limiting beliefs. And it's as simple to do as saying three words.

Dr. Ihaleakala Hew Len taught me that simply saying "I love you" to the Divine (or God, life, Tao, or whatever you want to call that superpower we're all in and of) could trigger a healing. This method of prayer or petition is from a Hawaiian spirituality called *ho'oponopono*. I won't describe the entire method to you here, as I wrote *Zero Limits* to do that. But let me describe how this works so you can use this clearing method right now.

The basic assumption is that every action you take is coming from inspiration or memory. Inspiration is a signal direct from the Divine. Memory is a program in your subconscious.

Everyone is coming from memory virtually all of the time. The task is to clean those memories so you can act from inspired signals from the Divine instead.

In other words, how you respond to these very words in this book is most likely a reaction based on memory. If you disagree with me, it's because you have an old program in your mind that is not jibing with my writing. If you agree with me, it may be because you have an old program that is in alignment with what I am saying. Either way, you aren't here with much objectivity and clarity, because there is baggage in the way. That baggage is memory. To clear it, you may need to say "I love you."

According to Dr. Hew Len, simply saying "I love you" to the Divine begins a clearing or cleansing process. The words stir the feelings within you. Those same words are heard by the Divine, which then sends down a signal to clean any memories in the way of being here in this moment with total clarity and awareness.

If you're hearing this concept for the first time, it may not make much sense to you. That's because you have an existing memory that conflicts with what I am sharing with you here. Your model of the world may not match this new model of the world. If you are feeling this confusion right now, simply hold it in your awareness and say "I love you" to the Divine (again, whatever that means to you).

While you're doing that, I'll say "I love you" as I write these words.

Dr. Hew Len's method involves cleaning yourself of all memories or negativity in order to see change in yourself and even in others. It seems bizarre, but when you take care of your own issues, they disappear in other people.

The whole idea is to love the problems away. You do it by saying "I love you" nonstop. There are three other statements you can say as well ("I'm sorry," "Please forgive me," and "Thank you"), but by far the three simple words in "I love you" are all you need. I've been doing it for three years now and my life is astonishing. I live in an almost moment-by-moment state of bliss.

Once I learned this method, I started to use it on everything that came up in me. I did the process in traffic jams, on the phone, in front of audiences, in the hot tub, smoking a cigar, walking, waiting in lines, feeling pain, recalling memories, and so forth. I would rarely say the three words out loud, but silently in my own mind. "I love you" became the new "chatter" in my mind. It transformed my life from one of worry to one of wonder.

Since I'm a practical metaphysician and an entrepreneur, I also wanted to see if this wild method would work on sales and other bottom-line results. Whenever I would write an article or sales letter I would send love into it. Whenever I would write another book—like my new one, *Zero Limits*, or even this one—I would keep saying "I love you" in my mind.

What I noticed was my e-mails and articles would get read and distributed to millions of people. And my book, *Zero Limits*, became an Amazon best seller—six months *before* it was published. So many people preordered it that it went on the Amazon best-seller list.

But I didn't stop there in my testing.

Because I want to be sure this method works for others and not just me, I taught it to my close friends. Bill Hibbler, coauthor with me of the book *Meet and Grow Rich*, was skeptical. But he borrowed a prepublication copy of *Zero Limits*, read it, and started loving his products and his list of subscribers. Here's what he said:

"Sales for January 1st to 4th were 41.39 percent higher than for December 1st to 4th. During the four-day period in January, I didn't mail my list or launch any new promotion during that time. All I did was clean while reading your book and throughout the day."

Bill went on to tell me he saw sales increase from sites like http://create-ultimate-ebooks.com/—which he wasn't promoting *at all*.

How is this possible?

How can cleaning yourself with a mantra like "I love you" make a difference in your sales?

It appears that there is nothing out there. The entire world is a projection of what you feel inside. So, if you feel love, you will attract love. Because love contains gratitude, you attract more things to be grateful for. This is the essence of my book *The Attractor Factor*, and of course of the movie *The Secret*. You get what you feel.

That's it.

At heart I think you (I) just want love. Well, so does everyone else. When you say "I love you" inside yourself, you cleanse yourself and you radiate an energy that others feel. The result: more sales.

Still skeptical?

Look at it this way:

Even if this whole method seems totally crazy to you, what harm can come from you saying "I love you" in your mind as you make calls, write e-mails, deliver pitches, and go about your day? If nothing else, you'll have better-feeling days.

Try it and see.
By the way, "I love you."

Here's an example of how this process works:

When I discovered that I had swollen lymph nodes in my chest that could potentially be cancer, I at first panicked. The cancer specialist I went to see painted a dark picture. He wanted to do an immediate biopsy, not even telling me of the long-term potential harm such a thing could do. I mentioned earlier in this book that I sent a call for help to close friends, healers, and others. They offered suggestions and I acted on many of them. But I also did this "I love you" cleansing method.

As I lay on my bed at home and silently said "I love you" over and over again in my mind to the Divine, I suddenly had an inspiration. It occurred to me that this health challenge, whatever it might be, was a gift. If it were, I wondered what it would be giving me. Many people have said their cancer or other health scare turned out to be the very thing that awakened them or strengthened them. I wondered if this problem had a gift for me.

I lay there, saying "I love you" in my mind, and then began to picture the swollen nodes in my chest. I had seen the film image of the scan, so I knew what they looked like. As I viewed them in my imagination, I began to talk to them. I asked, "What do you want me to learn?" and "What do you want to tell me?"

Almost instantly I saw an image of my late wife. She had passed away three years earlier. We had been married over 20 years and she was my best friend. As I remembered her, saw the image, and said "I love you," I began to feel grief. When she died, I cried every day for the next year. Then I cried every so often, and slowly it passed. But I still missed her.

I began to sense that the swollen nodes were a symbol for holding on to her. The actual film image of the nodes looked like a tiny creature hanging on to the inside of me. It seemed to be a solid metaphor for what I was holding on in my mind. I hadn't totally let go of my wife. A part of me was keeping her in me.

I continued to say "I love you" in my mind. As I did, other phrases surfaced, such as "I'm sorry" and "Please forgive me." As I continued to do this, I saw the images of the nodes get smaller, and smaller, and then finally disappear.

After 20 minutes or so of doing this cleansing method, I felt clear. While I couldn't yet prove that the swollen nodes were now gone, I knew inside myself that they were. I had loved them, heard their message, and let them go. And when I later had my MRI to look at those nodes, they were shown to now be harmless.

Just the other day I met a schoolteacher from San Antonio. He works with children with special needs. He read *Zero Limits* and began to practice the "I love you" meditation. He told me that one student was almost catatonic. The child would simply stare, with drool coming out his mouth, and would not respond.

The schoolteacher decided not to work with the child but to work on himself. He sat in the classroom and quietly repeated "I love you" while thinking of the child. He did this for several minutes.

He then went over to the student and asked him if he wanted to work on a math problem. To the teacher's amazement, the child looked at him and said, "Yes, I'll try that now."

The student then proceeded to work at his desk for the next 30 minutes. According to the teacher, this was an unheard-of breakthrough. He attributed the entire event to this cleansing method. Instead of working on the student, which is trying to change the outer, he worked on himself. Once he did, the child changed.

This is the miracle of this single method.

Think of something or someone in your life right now who still frustrates you. It could be a health problem. It could be a fellow worker you don't get along with. It doesn't matter what it is. Choose something, anything, to do this exercise.

As you hold that thing or person in your awareness, silently begin saying "I love you." You can direct the statement to the Divine. Whether you believe this is working or not, trust the process and continue it. All you have to do is repeat "I love you." As you do, you will begin to feel love, and you will begin to transform the thing or person.

Keep in mind that no one has to know you are doing anything at all. As Dr. Hew Len might say, there is no "out there." It's all in you. It's all about your relationship to the Divine. And all you have to do to clean up that relationship is say three little words.

Do that now and then record your experience here or in your journal:

# Clearing Method #6

## Tap-Dancing Your Troubles Away

*The cause of all negative emotions is a disruption in the body's energy system.*

—Gary Craig

Years ago I used to suffer from panic attacks. They were neither expected nor pleasant. Before I knew that I was creating them for unconscious reasons, I scrambled to find ways to eliminate them. One of the best tools for cleansing myself of those fears was so simple it seemed impossible.

Roger Callahan taught me the process. He called it Thought Field Therapy (TFT). One of his first products was an audio and video set called *Eliminate Fear of Public Speaking*. It involved tapping certain parts of your face, chest, and arm with your fingers. As you tapped, you would repeat phrases. While I didn't really believe (but sure hoped) his method would work, I did it anyway. To my amazement, it *did* work. And still works. Every time.

I began to study Thought Field Therapy, and then the children it produced, such as Emotional Freedom Techniques (EFT). Today there are hundreds of EFT teachers out there, and thousands who practice the method. One of them is Brad Yates.

Brad and I created a seminar called Money Beyond Belief (www.moneybeyondbelief.com). It taught people to do this simple tapping method to get clear of the unconscious beliefs surrounding money. He was also a guest on my seminar on how to attract a new car (www.attractanewcar.com). Again, Brad helped people get clear of their inner limitations so they

85

could allow and attract a new car into their lives. Since Brad is a master at EFT, I asked him to explain how you can do it right now, for anything you feel blocked with. Here's what he has to say:

## Clearing with EFT

### By Brad Yates

*www.bradyates.net*

In the process of manifesting one's desires, an often-overlooked part of the process is clearing. Most of the teachings on the Law of Attraction tell you to focus on what you really want, get in touch with the positive feelings, and then let go and watch it all show up.

And many people are left waiting and watching, getting more and more frustrated as it *doesn't* show up.

The problem is that 80 to 90 percent of our thinking is unconscious. So while we may have the occasional moment of focusing with positive energy on what we want—thinking that we really are in vibrational harmony with it—most of the time we are subject to what our internal thoughts and feelings are about what we can or should have. If you want to know what you internally are in harmony with having, look around at what you have. If it's not what you say you want, then most of the time you are not in vibrational harmony with what you say you want.

The good news is that this doesn't mean it doesn't work for you. The Law of Attraction is always working for you. It means that you have conflicting beliefs about what you want—and these can be cleared.

There are many methods for clearing these unconscious limiting beliefs. After the *Oprah* show about *The Secret*, Jack Canfield mentioned a few of these, including Emotional Freedom Techniques (EFT), which is my tool of choice. It is used to clear uncomfortable feelings—both emotional and physical. It is simple, effective, and usually very quick, and works at the level of the mind-body connection. Perhaps most important—you can easily do it on your own. A growing number of people are finding EFT to be an invaluable tool for gaining access to activating the Law of Attraction in a more conscious way—clearing the unconscious conflicts.

EFT is based on ancient Chinese medicine, using the same energy pathways, called meridians, as are used in acupuncture. Negative emotions—such as those that block us from attracting what we consciously say we want—are caused by disruption in this energy system. By tapping on key points, we balance the energy and clear the blocks. It is also the easiest stress-reduction tool I've ever found.

The universe has unlimited abundance—you can have whatever you want. The extent to which you do not experience anything you want is the extent to which you are resisting it. The most common reasons we resist abundance are that we either fear it is not safe for us or fear that we do not deserve it. Often it is a combination of the two.

Here are some suggestions for you to start using EFT to clear these limiting beliefs. Simply put, you will be using two fingers to lightly tap certain points where the meridians are more effectively stimulated. The first is the karate-chop spot on the side of your other hand. Then the points to tap are:

- The beginning of your eyebrow.
- The side of your eye.
- Right under your eye.

(continued)

- Right under your nose.
- Right under your mouth (top of the chin).
- Right where your collarbones come together.
- Four inches below your underarm.
- The top of your head.

For more information on how to do EFT, including a diagram and audio instruction, please visit www.bradyates.net and click on "EFT."

Begin by closing your eyes, taking a deep breath, and asking yourself, "How safe is it for me to have _____ (whatever particular form of abundance you are wanting, i.e., a new car, a house, etc.)?" Notice what feeling comes up in your body, as well as any thoughts about why you shouldn't have this. Rate the resistance on a scale of 0 to 10.

Tap on the side of your hand (karate-chop point), and state: "Even though it doesn't feel safe to have this, I deeply and completely love and accept myself."

Then tap through the various points, stating: "It's not safe for me to have this."

Take a deep breath, and check in with yourself to see if the resistance feels lessened. Keep repeating until you feel relief.

Now rate yourself on a scale of 0 to 10 on how much you feel/believe you deserve to have what you want, and do the same exercise with the statement: "Even though I don't feel I deserve to have this, I deeply and completely love and accept myself."

You may be asking, "Why would I want to say that? I'm supposed to focus only on the positive!"

So I'll ask you: If you spilled something on your floor, would it be wise to ignore it, and from that point forward just focus on where the floor is clean? Could you really wipe the mess out of your mind if you don't wipe it up? Right—clean it up, clear it out, and give yourself the freedom to move about wherever you want without having to pretend something isn't there.

As you clear the limiting beliefs, you give yourself the freedom to be in vibrational harmony with what you truly want even when you aren't consciously trying to do so—which is naturally going to be the majority of the time.

One last thing: EFT can also be a very effective tool for clearing when used with other methods. I have even incorporated it with ho'oponopono, tapping the various points while stating, "I'm sorry, please forgive me, thank you, I love you." Give it a try.

For a more in-depth look at clearing blocks with EFT, check out *Money Beyond Belief* by Joe and me at www.moneybeyond-belief.com. Even if money isn't what you want to create more of, the same issues that block money will often block whatever else you may not yet be allowing yourself to enjoy. You deserve abundance—allow it.

*Clearing Method #7*

# Nevillize It

*The world is the human imagination pushed out.*

—Neville Goddard

One of the most powerful tools for attracting what you want and removing anything in the way of it getting to you is something I call "Nevillizing." I coined the term to pay homage to Neville Goddard, a Barbados mystic who spoke often and wrote many books, such as *Your Faith Is Your Fortune*, *The Power of Awareness*, *Immortal Man*, and *At Your Command*.

Neville believed you create your reality through your imagination. If you wanted to change something in your life, you did it with a new imagined experience. But Neville was quick to point out that imagery alone wasn't enough. You have to do two more things: You also have to feel the end result and feel it as if it had already happened.

Most people think that what they see in their mind will tend to come about. But to accelerate the process of manifestation, you must also feel what it would be like to already have the thing achieved. In other words, seeing the new car you want is one thing. Imagining what it would feel like to *already have it* is quite another. The latter speeds up the Law of Attraction.

In a talk Neville gave in 1969, he said:

"See a situation as something on the outside, and you become entangled in its shadows—for everyone who responds to your imaginal act is a shadow. How can a shadow be causative in your world? The moment you give another the power of causation, you have transferred to him the power that rightfully belongs to you. Others are only shadows, bearing witness to the activities taking place in you. The world is a mirror, forever reflecting what you are doing within yourself."

What Neville taught is that your outer world is simply a projection of your inner world. Change the inner and you change the outer. If you want to attract anything, you do it on the inner plane of your being. You do it with imagination and feeling.

Here's an example of how this works:

When I was called to appear on the *Larry King Live* television show on CNN, I jumped at the chance. But I confess I was also nervous. I was about to go on live TV, seen by millions of people. All my fears and self-doubts kicked into gear. What if I say something stupid? What if I stutter? What if my mind goes blank? What if I choke? What if Larry doesn't like me? What if the viewers don't agree with me?

On the plane from Texas to Los Angeles, I sat and felt my fear. I realized that the more I imagined and felt what I didn't want, the more I was going to bring it into reality. I'd be implementing the Law of Attraction for what I didn't want to see happen.

What was I going to do?

Then I remembered Neville. I pulled out a pad, got out my pen, and began to script the TV show as I wanted it to happen. I saw myself with Larry King and described my feelings and the experience as if it had already happened. I made this written vision as complete as possible, infused it with energy and emotion, and began to feel that it was actually going to happen.

This took only a few minutes. When I was done, I read and reread the writing. Every time I did, I smiled. When I arrived at my hotel, I put the writing beside my pillow and looked at it often. The piece of writing became a touchstone reminding me of the end result I wanted. I would reread it, feel the joy of the show going the way I described it, and relax.

That evening, when I sat down before Larry King with the cameras on both of us, I felt calm and confident. I answered his questions, smiled, laughed, and even stunned Larry by announcing the making of a sequel to the movie *The Secret*. In short, I created a new experience by Nevillizing it.

You can do this, too. The idea is to write a script of what you want to happen, but to write it as if it had already happened. Pretend you are writing your diary entry for the end of the day when you attracted your goal. Get into the good feelings. Imagine the joy you will feel. This simple exercise will program the event to come your way.

For example, what if you want a new house? Wallace Wattles, writing in *The Science of Getting Rich*, said: "Live in the new house, mentally, until it takes form around you physically. In the mental realm, enter at once into full enjoyment of the things you want."

Wattles went on to advise, "See the things you want as if they were actually around you all the time; see yourself as owning and using them."

Both Wattles and Neville were advising you to use your imagination now to create the future you want. But the trick is to do it with feeling, not just mental imagery. I think this is another missing secret in the quest for attracting what you want: Too many people just use their mental imagery skills and forget to add the power of emotion to their imagination. Feeling accelerates the process of attraction. This is why you tend to attract the things you love or hate. The intense emotions step on the gas.

Neville once said, "Right now you are playing a part. If you don't like it you can change it. You could play the part of a man wealthier than you were 24 hours ago. It's only a part for you to play, if you desire it."

The way to change the part you are playing is through this form of role-playing with feeling. You imagine how you want a situation to be, but imagine it with feeling, and as if it has already passed. Doing this will also help you know what action to take, if any, to begin to attract your desired result to you.

Neville wrote in *The Power of Awareness*:

> You must assume the feeling of the wish fulfilled until your assumption has all the sensory vividness of reality. You must imagine that you are already experiencing what you desire. That is, you must assume the feeling of the fulfillment of your desire until you are possessed by it and this feeling crowds all other ideas out of your consciousness.

That's what I'm going to ask you to do in a moment—write a scenario with such detail that it feels real, and it feels as if it already happened. Keep in mind that the event itself may still be different from what you describe when you Nevillize it. You're still learning how to attract what you want. So am I. What you are doing here is learning how to consciously create circumstances.

In the space that follows, or in your journal, Nevillize something you want to attract. Be sure you paint the picture of what you want. Your focus is on your desired outcome. You are a scriptwriter for your own dreams. The only tool you need is a pen and your energized imagination. Have fun!

_____

_____

_____

_____

_____

_____

_____

_____

_____

_____

_____

_____

_____

_____

_____

_____

_____

_____

_____

_____

_____

_____

# Please Forgive Me

*Don't ask yourself what the world needs. Ask yourself what makes you come alive and then go do that. Because what the world needs is people who have come alive.*

—Howard Thurman

If you feel stuck in any area of your life, if you're not attracting the car, house, job, mate, or anything else you really want, it could very well be due to a lack of forgiveness.

Maybe you didn't forgive the other person. Maybe you didn't forgive yourself. It doesn't matter. Holding on to past emotions, memories, or stories is guaranteed to tie up your energy and block your ability to attract what you want.

What you have to do now is forgive.

I used to struggle with this one. I was afraid that if I forgave someone, I would not learn the lesson they gave me and I would be suckered again. But as I looked at that belief, I realized it was just that: a belief. It wasn't reality. It wasn't factual. It wasn't true.

I remember when a client owed me a great deal of money. He wasn't paying, and it was clear he was going to rob me of what was due to me. In those days my mind-set was still that of a victim. I thought my client, and much of the world, was out to get me. I had read so many books about robber barons in history, and about survival of the fittest, that I felt unless I became greedy and cutthroat in business, I'd always fail. However, I refused to become something I didn't like.

I refused to become one of "them." So I lived with my pain and resentment.

Of course, the only person this hurt was me. The client who owed me money never felt my pain. I have no idea if he felt anything at all. So my holding a grudge kept only one person down: me.

As I began to read self-help books and use some of the clearing methods you've been reading about in this book, I began to realize that I could let go of my resentment. I could forgive my client. I could forgive myself.

I did just that. And—you probably guessed it—my client surfaced and paid me the money he owed me. But I didn't forgive in order to collect the money. I forgave and forgot and let it go.

But let's look at this more closely so you understand forgiveness and the power of it as a clearing method.

Forgiving another person is, in part, an ego trip. When you say "I forgive you" to someone, you are saying you had some sort of hold over them. You were the King or Queen, and by the "I forgive you" decree you could pronounce them "free" of your resentment. That's not forgiveness. It may even be a form of manipulation.

What's more powerful is to say "I'm sorry" to the people you hurt. If you've never seen the television show My Name Is Earl, watch it sometime. It's about a petty thief who awakens to the idea that if he does good things, good things happen. He makes a list of everyone he ever hurt in his life. He then works to do something to erase his wrong.

A couple of decades ago I did something similar. I made a list of people I felt I had hurt. I then went to them and paid them money if I owed it, returned tools or objects if I had walked off with them, and told them I was sorry for my behavior. I did my best to make peace with my past. It was a wonderful feeling.

I also know there is a level of forgiveness beyond being forgiven by others or forgiving others. The forgiveness that becomes one of the most powerful clearing methods you can use in an instant is the one where you forgive *yourself*.

It's your perception of a situation or person that is an error. It's not the other person. Yes, they may have done something you prefer they hadn't done. But it's your judgment of them that causes the friction. When you let go of your judgment, you free yourself. And often, when you free yourself, the other person does what you wanted all along. But your motivation has to come from forgiveness of you.

In many ways, this might be called radical forgiveness. It's the understanding that nothing bad happened. You may have judged it as bad. But from the Divine's view of the world, what occurred is simply what occurred. It's over. It's done. It's history. Holding on to your judgments about the person or event is burning up your own energy—energy that could be working to attract what you want to you.

Colin Tipping, author of the book *Radical Forgiveness*, writes:

> Traditional forgiveness is "letting bygones be bygones." And that's OK as far as it goes. However, because we believe that

something bad happened, we still think of ourselves as having been victimized no matter how hard we try to forgive. It can only play itself out as a struggle between two conflicting energies: the need to condemn versus the desire to forgive.

In Tipping's view, "radical forgiveness" is when you realize nothing bad or negative or evil happened at all. In fact, what happened didn't happen *to* you but *for* you. It happened to help you awaken and to grow. It was part of the curriculum to bring you where you are now. And from where you are, you can attract miracles.

Obviously, the thing to do is forgive.

But how do you do that?

Just saying "I forgive myself" may not cause the shift inside yourself that you seek. And you don't need to say "I forgive you" to anyone, as they weren't at fault to begin with. They were simply acting out their own programs, and the two of you created a story to help you grow. In fact, you probably should *thank* the other person.

Again, how do you forgive yourself?

I'm going to draw from my book *Zero Limits*, and suggest that what you need to do is ask the Divine to forgive you for your errors in judgment. This can be as simple a process as saying "Please forgive me" or "I'm sorry." You don't need to say this out loud. You don't need to feel it, either. As you silently repeat the phrases, directing them to the Divine (whatever that means to you), you begin the process of releasing the stuck energy inside yourself.

This is not complicated. You do not have to understand how it works. You are working on a soul level to release the hold within yourself that your judgments have created. Try it and see. Say "I'm sorry" and "Please forgive me" to your sense of the Divine. Then get silent and allow the silence to free you.

You might also make a list of people or events that need forgiveness, which you can write here or in your journal.

_____

_____

_____

_____

_____

_____

_____

_____

_____

_____

_____

_____

_____

And remember to forgive yourself!

# Clearing Method #9

## Your Body Speaks

*In order to attain a thing it is necessary that the mind should fall in love with it.*

—William Walter Atkinson

When I was on the *Larry King Live* television show the second time, Larry asked me, "Can the ideas in the movie *The Secret* help an addict?"

"Yes," I told him. "Thousands of people are already helped by it."

"But an addict?" Larry persisted. "An addict's body is still addicted, isn't it?"

I went on to say that your mind is not just in your brain but throughout your body. Your brain is the operating system or control center, but your mind isn't just there. Your mind is actually *throughout* your body. As a result, you can hold stuck memories and locked emotions in your body. Free your body and you free your mind. Free your mind and you free your body.

"Change your mind and you change your body," I told Larry.

Because of the sound bite nature of all television shows, I didn't get any more of a chance to elaborate on my answers. Thank goodness for books like this one, and for people like Jennifer McLean, who wrote the following article to help you clear your body/mind of any stuck issues. Jennifer has trained in three disciplines of healing: craniosacral, polarity, and Reiki therapies. She has been practicing these modalities of healing in private sessions with individuals and in workshop environments for 15 years (www.healingrelease.com).

## Clearing the Old Debris of Trauma and Leftover Energy Blocks

### By Jennifer McLean

The techniques that follow will take you on a journey into the body intelligence to unmask the thoughts stuck in physical cellular energy systems. These stuck thoughts keep us from our dreams and show up as pain (physical, emotional, and spiritual).

The body often holds blocks as thoughts and emotions, collected in the tissue to be discovered, acknowledged, and released. The energies that get stuck in the body are often a consequence of an unresolved trauma. The trauma may have resulted from physical, emotional, mental, or spiritual injury, but in my experience a combination if not all of those are involved for the energy to be stuck. For example, a physical trauma can be as dramatic as a car accident or as minor as kicking your brother and hurting your toe. What is most important is the thought behind the action, or the thought that occurred as you were receiving the trauma and where that thought got trapped in the body. When the thought and emotion behind the physical energy block is revealed, acknowledged, and released in gratitude, the body's natural healing intelligence takes over, repatterning the body into balance, health, and flow. When in the flow, the floodgates of opportunity open.

I have often experienced, both in my own process and in the work I do with my clients, that when I go to the body and "ask into" the cellular structure and the emotions that are held in those structures, the block is easier to get at. For example, I have worked with visualization and feeling the feelings of abundance, joy, relationship, and so on with mixed results. When I take those same feelings into the body and ask into the body where these might reside, I will be shown the path to understanding and/or releasing both the block and the true feeling sense—both physically and emotionally—of what I wanted.

## The Body Journey—Techniques for Healing Release

I liken these techniques to quantum physics and the "observer effect." The focus is appreciating your energetic system as it expresses itself. As you watch the energetic movement and patterns of the blocks and releases, the body knows that you are paying attention and alters and reorganizes into a new system or pattern of renewed health and balance. It is an active dialogue:

> *You:* Hi, body, show me what you want to show me, and I promise to be present and listen.

> *Body:* Oh, cool, you're here. I have heard your request for abundance/relationship/freedom/fun/happiness (etc.), and boy, do I have some things to show you about that.

It has already started: The technique and the words you are about to read to describe it have been infused with forgiveness, love, and balance. As you read, it the process has already started and the body is preparing to receive you.

*Technique Number 1: Healing Through Trauma*

Read through this technique once before you try it.

(continued)

*Part One—Find Your Center*    Find a comfortable place, either lying or sitting with your back supported. Take several (three minimum) very deep breaths with the intention of oxygenating your body and relaxing. Each breath should be 10 seconds or longer. The breath starts just below the belly button, which is the first to rise (you can put your hand there to check); the chest rises second, and the shoulders rise (slightly) last. Imagine the last of the inward breath filling the very uppermost part of your lungs. At the top of that breath it should feel as if you are giving your shoulders and neck an internal massage.

Now, from this point of relaxation, go inside your body and find the place that feels like it is your center. Drift down into your body like a pearl sinking slowly and gently in water. Where the pearl stops, that is your center. Find the stillest point in this center point. If thoughts wander in, fold them as if they were pieces of cloth and lay them aside.

*Part Two—Look, Notice, Feel, Dialogue*    Once your center space feels clear, go to where there is physical pain; go to the tension and/or discomfort in your body. This pain is calling you for a reason and is most relevant to what you want to address.

When I say "go to," I mean take your attention to that place in your body. Pretend your eyes are inside your body and you can see inside this place of tension and pain. This is the most important piece of this technique: going to it and observing it. What does it look like? Some see an object (glass, cylinder, box, house, toy, etc.); some see a color; some have a feeling sense (soft, hard, gooey, etc.); for some it is an emotion (anger, frustration, confusion, etc.).

Having brought your complete attention to this place inside your body, take a close look and start your internal dialogue. Describe in detail to yourself what you are seeing and feeling in that place of tension or pain. Notice if it changes, and observe the change. (Remember the observer effect: Your body is happy to see you here and wants to show you something. It will use a language of symbols that you will understand.) Ask into it:

- Why are you (the thing you are observing) here?

- What is this about?

- Do you have something in particular to show me? (Notice if it changes, and ask why it changed.)

- How has having this (shape, feeling, sound, sense) served me?

- Where do you come from (an event, an uncomfortable conversation, a physical injury, some abusive incident, etc.)? (*Special Note:* If it is a traumatic event, don't go back into the trauma; just acknowledge the memory and go back to what you have been observing with the new understanding that this tension and pain are a result of that incident.)

- Am I willing to release this? If so, how can I resolve or release this? (You are not looking for an "exercise more" or a "lose weight" kind of answer here. The answer is in the moment with the object you are observing. What does releasing this thing look like or feel like in your body at that moment?)

- Is there something here that can help me to release you (the thing you are observing)? (There are helpers available to assist you with this; ask for guidance, help, tools, etc. to manage whatever you are looking at.)

Now watch the changes as you have a conversation with this aspect of your body. It will shift and change and find a pattern of balance. When the shift occurs, it might feel like a big sigh,

(*continued*)

tears may come, or laughing may occur. There is often heat released and sometimes it may feel like it is pulsing. Gurgling in the colon is also evidence of shifting energies. These are all forms of energetic release.

As whatever you are observing shifts and releases, notice the rest of your body. Is there tension somewhere else? It is like peeling an onion; one release opens the opportunity for a new area that was likely related to that area of blockage to reveal itself. Or that area may be connected to another part of the body; go to that new place that is calling you and do the exercise again.

I recommend finishing this exercise using Joe's and Dr. Hew Len's ho'oponopono technique. Thank it, apologizing to it for having the experience that led to this block, and loving the person who created the block (you) and the person you have become who is now able to release it.

*Examples*   So that you really get this and feel more comfortable with the technique, I will walk you through some examples of what this technique could look like.

I have a pain in my lower back on the left. I have done the breathing techniques and have found the stillness at my center moving from there to where the pain is in my back. My attention is focused on the point of pain, and it looks dark and uninviting. It feels angry and indifferent at the same time. I see a mixture of red and black. As I observe this I notice my colon is feeling heavier and is moving and changing. I ask the place in my back why is it there: What does it need to show me? It responds with more indifference and a sense that it is turning its back on me. I ask again: I am here, I am listening, I am no longer ignoring you, and what can I do for you? It melts into sadness and reveals that the anger and frustration are just a front to hide the sadness. I ask what is this sadness, why is it here, and how is it serving me? It tells me that I am so much more than what I have been showing to the outside world. It tells me that every time I am holding the sadness instead of feeling it, there will be pain and tension in my back; it is my barometer of being authentic and in the world.

Another client's experience: Marcia's ankle was hurt in an injury five years earlier and has never quite healed. She goes inside and brings her attention and awareness to the ankle. The ankle says to look at the knee first. She goes to the knee and senses a defensive energy that looks like a physical square block: hard, cold, and metallic. Marcia asks what is it, and why is it there? It starts to lighten in color and her ankle starts to hurt. The box turns into her bedroom when she was five years old and her brother is bothering her to the point of fear of personal injury.

She sees the box now as the hard, cold, steely feeling she had toward her brother. She sees that five-year-old girl kick her brother really hard, resulting in her toe, ankle, and knee being hurt. (She had completely forgotten this incident.) She is also shown that this defensive yet aggressive posture that is still stuck in her tissue as cellular memory is keeping her from many people and new opportunities in her life. The box is still there, so she asks if there is a tool or helper to release it. She is handed a jackhammer, which she uses to break up the block. She is then given a powerful vacuum that sucks out the leftover debris. She is left with an open, clear space and is guided to fill it with light.

The whole leg released during the cleaning and clearing phase and became straighter and stronger. She has not experienced any more pain in the ankle. Once this incident was released from her cells, her life opened up; she took a less defensive posture in her relationships and was more in the moment and in the flow.

Use this technique weekly or even daily if it feels right.

(continued)

*Technique Number 2: The Negative Story Process*

We all have stories. Sometimes we dwell on those stories: Someone—your parents, your friends, your boss—"done you wrong." We dwell on these negative incidents because they are often still stuck in our bodies. When old negative thinking and debris are stuck in various energy blocks in our bodies, they act like big rocks in the river of our lives and slow down the energy flow. When the energy flow is blocked, we get sick and feel physical pain or emotional pain and mental fatigue (memory loss, etc.). This lack of flow is a mirror for the lack of good flowing to us.

The opportunity is to get clear of our stories, to take each moment and look at what we are feeling emotionally and how that is showing up in our bodies. Our bodies are perfect diagnostic tools for our emotional and unconscious states of habitual dysfunction.

- Tell yourself your negative story or victimhood, but you have only one or two minutes to tell it!

- Using the internal body observational techniques you learned in the preceding discussion, what does that story feel like in your body? Feel it. Where in your body are you feeling this negative emotion? Feel that.

- Now say to yourself, "I don't want to feel this anymore."

- Next ask yourself, "What do I *want* to feel?" Connect and anchor into your solar plexus and heart area to help identify what it is you want to feel.

- Move this new positive feeling sense from your mind (where most of us think we are feeling) into your body. What does it feel like in your body to have the new positive energies that you want? What does it feel like in your body to feel peace, to feel joy, to feel confidence, to feel abundance? Where in your body do you feel these glorious energies? Stay in your body and really feel these new positive energies.

- Take it to the next level now and describe what your life looks like with these feelings. Use the anchored feeling you discovered in your body to anchor it into a story, a visualization of your life and how it appears when you are really congruent with these positive energies, and how your body feels in these new energies.

- Take that story of what you want back into your body again and feel it.

This is the Law of Attraction in action; when you are talking about your old stories and still being victimized by them in your mind, you are reinforcing that energy and attracting more of it. Use this exercise to move yourself into what you really want, and to use your body as the anchor for those feelings, creating a momentum of good rushing toward you.

# Clearing Method #10

## The Vital Message

*Body is the materialization of mind.*

—Lester Levenson

About 20 years ago I learned a clearing method that I still use today. I've taught it to a few others and they still use it as well. I'm going to reveal how to do it in this chapter, so you will have this method in your back pocket to pull out and use whenever you don't feel clear.

The method itself is simple. In my experience whenever you aren't clear, you feel it. The feeling isn't comfortable. It may be sensed as anger, frustration, impatience, unhappiness, depression, sadness, apathy, or any other lower-energy emotion. It's this feeling that brings you down. But it's this same feeling that can bring you up—and to even higher states of awareness and greater power to attract what you want.

Here's how it works:

1. You have a feeling you don't particularly like. Again, it's any variation of unhappiness. Sometimes people will say, "I'm not unhappy, I'm just angry!" Well, obviously, anger is a form of unhappiness. Whatever the description for you, welcome it.

2. Sit with the feeling, allowing it to be there. Far too often we want to get rid of the emotion we don't like. We try to drown it in alcohol or eat it away with food. The variety of escapes we have is enormous. Some people go jogging. Others go shopping. Some sit and sulk. Others throw

things. The suggestion here is to do nothing but *sit with the feeling*. I know this is uncomfortable, but this is the door to freedom.

3.  Describe the feeling. When you have a headache, instead of reaching for some medicine, stay with the headache. Keep your attention on it by describing it to yourself. How big is it? How wide is it? What color is it? How deep is it? There are no right or wrong answers to these questions. They are asked to keep your mind focused on the pain or the feeling. As you do so, something amazing will happen: The pain or feeling will begin to disappear.

4.  Finally, ask the feeling what it is trying to tell you. I've referred to this tip in other areas of this book. Your emotion is there for a reason. There's a lesson to be learned. *Get the lesson, and you no longer need the experience.* What I do is get quiet, close my eyes, focus on the feeling—even if I dread it—and let it speak to me. This may feel like a mind game to you, but the answers you receive could also be the difference between pain and pleasure, failure and success.

These four steps are a breeze to do. Essentially you are simply allowing the stuck feeling to stay long enough to hear the message it has for you. Once you get the message, you're clear. It's really that easy.

Here's an example of how I recently used this clearing method:

I'm a lifetime member of the Society of American Magicians (SAM). Before a monthly meeting of the local chapter of SAM, I was asked to perform a magic trick. Now, performing magic for family and friends is one thing. Performing for professional magicians is quite another.

All my fears kicked in. I began to dread the meeting. I spent three days trying to decide what magic trick to perform, one good enough to baffle these accomplished magicians. Nothing I rehearsed pleased me. I even spent money to buy more magic effects—when I already have tens of thousands of dollars' worth of magic in a spare room in my home.

After spending all this time being unhappy, I started to entertain ways to get out of the meeting. I didn't *have* to go, I told myself. No one was paying me. No one was really expecting me to perform. It was simply an invitation I could accept or refuse. I started to feel I should refuse it and just not attend the meeting.

But my rule of thumb is this: If I fear it, I must do it.

With that decision made, I now had to deal with my feelings. They were getting dark and heavy. I started to feel ill. My left ear started to ache. I felt myself getting a little depressed.

This was not good.

I then remembered this clearing method, which I call the Vital Message, for the very reason that you want to hear the vital message the emotion is trying to give you. I knew once I heard it, I would be free.

The sense of dread was there. I could feel it in my body. I didn't like it. I could have chosen to ignore it, repress it, bury it, or any number of escapes. Instead, I chose to sit with it. I allowed the feeling to be there. No judgment. No challenge. No mind games.

After a few minutes of being quiet, just feeling this sense of dread, I suddenly remembered the first time I ever called a magician. I was a child, probably not even 12 years old. I had gotten the phone number of a magician in a large city near me and called him. This was my introduction to a real magician, someone doing what I had fantasized about doing.

The magician answered the phone, but he was crying. He had just learned, only minutes before my call, that his mother had died. I had no idea how to respond. I was a kid. I didn't have social skills. I didn't know about death. I didn't know what to say. As far as I can remember, I simply said good-bye and forgot about the experience.

But my unconscious had not forgotten. That first touch with real magic tainted my relationship with magic for the rest of my life—until the day I allowed my emotion to express itself.

What my feeling of dread said to me was, "You expect all magicians to think you show up at the wrong time and say and do the wrong thing."

Once I received this vital message, the feeling left me. It simply evaporated. It was no longer there. It was as though I needed to look at that childhood experience with adult eyes and realize what happened then was not true for all times. Once I let it go, I was free.

In case you are wondering, I did go to that magicians meeting. I gave a very informal talk about magic and marketing. I also performed a mind-reading effect. The crowded room of my peers loved the presentation, applauded numerous times throughout, laughed at my jokes, and came up afterwards and congratulated me.

That's real magic. And it came from listening to the message in my emotion.

In the following spaces, or in your journal, take an emotion you may have, or had recently, and walk through these four steps.

1. What is the feeling?

    _____
    _____
    _____
    _____

2. Can you simply sit with the feeling for a few minutes?

    _____
    _____
    _____
    _____

3. What is a description of the feeling? (How big is it? Where is it? What color is it? How deep is it?)

    _____
    _____
    _____
    _____
    _____
    _____
    _____
    _____
    _____
    _____

4. What is the message from the feeling? (Make it up if you want. Your pretend answer may be more relevant than you think.)

# Part Three

## The Miracles

*Verily, it is easier for a camel to pass through the eye of a needle than for a scientific man to pass through a door.*

—Sir Arthur Eddington, physicist

# A Miracles Coaching Q & A

## An Excerpt from a Miracles Coaching Teleseminar

LEE: I'm Lee Follender. I'm one of Dr. Joe Vitale's Miracles Coaches, and I'm thrilled to be here tonight. We're going to try something a little bit different on this call than we've been doing with our previous calls, and I wanted to kind of give you a little background on why.

One of the things we've noticed, or I certainly have noticed when I'm in a seminar, is that when someone else in the audience asks a question, it's really easy for me to see that there's something in it for me. For example, they ask a similar question to one that I would have asked, or it reminds me of something that I had a question about in the past. So that kind of synchronicity is something that sometimes can be missed when a person is speaking a monologue about a subject and we just listen. It seems like there's something available in being engaged in a dialogue that connects us at a deeper, kind of personal level. So I invite you, each and every one of you, to bring that level of engagement to our call tonight.

In working with my clients and talking with our mentor team, some of the questions, as you can imagine, can be pretty challenging. So we've decided to bring them along with the questions you sent in to the call for Joe to answer. And our intention is that tonight will provide you with some terrific insights into the work you're doing in creating a miraculous life. And whether you are new to the conversation or you've been working at it for a while, I think the wide range of questions we selected should be really helpful for you.

So whether you're a beginner, just starting your journey, or a more experienced traveler, sit back and make yourself comfortable, and I'm going to invite Joe Vitale to join us.

So we know you're there, Joe. Right?

JOE: I am indeed. I haven't left yet.

LEE: Okay. Good. So I'm going to give you our first question. Question number one: You're in the middle of your day, and a limiting belief comes up. You notice you're really upset. What do you do?

JOE: That's a great question, because that happened to me just today, and so I can reflect back and see what I did. And the first thing I did was acknowledge it.

I find that if I fight with it, I give it power. If I fight with it, I'm just continuing the process of keeping it in my awareness, and it just sticks with me like glue.

So I say, "Yup, there it is, it's a negative belief," and I feel it. It's important to feel it, because if you don't feel it, you can sometimes bury an emotion. But my experience has been you bury it alive, and what happens is it will reoccur; it may surface, and it may surface inappropriately. You may get angry at a certain point, or fall into tears at some point. You may just have some sort of emotional outburst at an inappropriate time, because you didn't feel the emotion originally.

So when I see the emotion or I feel the emotion, I recognize the emotion, and I allow it to be there. And I admit, I really don't want it. If it's something that makes me a little sad or angry in the moment, I prefer that it would leave. But if I feel it and say, "Yeah, it's there," and just totally be with it for a moment—and really all it takes is a moment—when you don't fight it, it dissipates. It dissolves. It evaporates.

Then the next thing I do is reach for a better thought. Because when the negative belief came in, who knows where it came from? It could have just bubbled into my awareness. It could have been something I read, something I heard; I saw a flash on the news, got a letter in the mail. Who knows what it was? But whatever it happened to be, it's okay. And I then reach for a thought that feels better. And that's really kind of my motto: to reach for a thought that feels good.

A belief that's bothering you—acknowledge it, feel it, express it, and let it go. Reach for the alternative to it. Reach for the opposite of it.

In my book *The Attractor Factor*, I say step one is to know what you don't want. Well, that belief that just came in is probably one you don't want.

And step two in *The Attractor Factor* is to choose what you do want, and one great way to do it is simply to reverse the belief you're not liking. So if there was a belief there that showed up like, well, a common one is *there's never enough*, or fill in the blank. There's never enough money, there's never enough food, there's never enough love, there's never enough (fill in the blank). So there's a common belief there's never enough. The opposite thought might be something like *there is more than enough* money to go around all the time for all people, or there's more than enough money for me to pay my bills when they're due, or even before they're due. So the point is you'll reach for a better belief. You choose that. You have control.

So that's what I would do, and that's what I do.

LEE: Okay. Great. And that really gives you something to actually do in the moment, instead of just being at the mercy of the thought or the belief.

JOE: You were a victim in the past. From this moment on, you cannot be a victim. I just told you how to reverse it. And now you're awakening. Now you have choice. And that's the beauty of all of this—this call, this whole program. You now have choice. You take back your power. And that is exhilarating.

LEE: That's great. Okay. Question two, what about babies? Do they attract what they have? You know, things like colic, gas, you know, or even serious things like birth defects or whatever?

JOE: Yeah. That question has been popping up. It's interesting. People are watching the movie *The Secret*. And if people on the call haven't seen it, go get it. Just go to Amazon. It's probably in bookstores now, or go to www. TheSecret.tv. Oprah has talked about *The Secret*. Larry King talked about it; I was on his show. Ellen DeGeneres has talked about it. *TIME* magazine did a story. *Newsweek* just did a story on it. So there is a buzz going on around the country, if not the globe, about the movie, which is all about the Law of Attraction. And now the skeptics and the people who are sincerely curious, they're questioning, and they are coming out of the woodwork.

LEE: Right.

JOE: And they're asking things like well, babies, do they attract this stuff to themselves? You know, if they're born innocently, and there are babies who even have strokes six weeks after birth, did they attract that? My position is they did, but like all of us, we attract it on an unconscious level.

When we get in a car accident, when we have anything happen so that we shake our head and think boy, that was terrible, and that somebody else did it to us, that's the illusion. The reality is we pull it in on an unconscious level. This is one of my main themes these days: that we're all about, including me, we're all about getting more and more conscious.

Well, babies all come in, it seems to me, with a certain programming. If you think about it, even twins, when they're born to a family, can be raised by the same parents, educated in the same school system, go to the same religious facility, and do all kind of social things together, but they can have very different personalities, and they seem to have come into the world with some of this.

So my feeling on this is that babies are coming in with some sort of programming. Part of it's personality, and part of it's genetics, and part of it's the physical experience. Where that began, I don't know. I think we can all ask God or Buddha or somebody else, at some point, because I don't know. But my position is yes, we all attract everything, including babies, but we're doing it unconsciously.

LEE: I got it. All right. If this is brand-new to someone (and we may have somebody new on the call; for example, I think we did speak to somebody who's just starting today)—

JOE: Yes.

LEE: —how do you start?

JOE: How do you start? Well, my favorite place to start is by playing with the idea of how would you like your life to be. I love that question. I love questions along the same lines, like how good can you stand it? What specifically would you like to have differently in your life?

And when I'm asking these questions, I want people to think of possibilities. I don't want them to think of problems.

Where all of this begins, with me, is with the idea of focusing on what you want.

Also, in *The Attractor Factor*, and I'm sure it's in the movie *The Secret*, and I've seen Oprah say this from time to time, intention rules the earth.

And so what I encourage people to do is to begin to state intentions. And what I mean by an intention, in case somebody doesn't know, is that's a declaration of how you want a particular outcome to be. And it could be something like you intend to have a certain body shape and be at a certain weight at a certain time; it could be that you intend to get a particular car of a particular make, model, and color; and it could be that you're looking for a position in a particular company. It could be that you're looking for a pay increase of so much money per month. I'm talking in generalities here, but in your mind, you should be speaking in very specific terms.

And stating intentions—declaring what you want and playing with possibilities of how you would like your life to be—begins the process of going in the direction of those very things. This is one of the things I find so amazing and miraculous and magical about life: When you state an intention, the first thing that happens is that your body and your mind get in alignment to go in the direction of that intention.

My favorite example is when you buy a new car. If you bought a Volkswagen, before you bought that Volkswagen, you just noticed them here and there. After you bought the Volkswagen, you saw them all over the place, and you probably thought there was an invasion of Volkswagens. Your mind had become alert to it, because you had focused on it.

When you focus on an intention, your mind and your body start to go in that direction. It's just a basic rule of psychology. You get more of whatever you focus on.

But also, metaphysically, the universe itself, the energy of all that is, seems to realign itself to bring your intention to you, and to put you in situations to make your intention come into being.

So I would say where you begin is playing with your intention. What do you want? How do you want life to be? How good can you stand your life? What do you want to really change? And again, you're focusing on possibilities, not on problems. You're focusing on your outcome, the way you want it. That, to me, is the juicy stuff. That's where it all begins.

LEE: Okay. Well, good. That kind of brings up the next question, which is somebody wanted to know: Why is it taking so long? You know, sometimes it seems easier to attract negative things than positive things. That's kind of two questions, but they're really similar in nature.

JOE: Yeah. Well, that's a great one. Both of them are great. You might have to remind me of the second. I'll take the first, first.

LEE: Why is it taking so long?

JOE: Okay. Why is it taking so long? I spoke last Sunday at the World Wellness Convention. (Read about it at http://themissingsecret.info.) Deepak Chopra spoke on Saturday night. I spoke on Sunday morning and had a standing-room-only crowd. In fact, there were people sitting on the floor, and there were a hundred or more standing outside the doors, because they couldn't get in, and it was just packed.

LEE: And I was there. It was great.

JOE: You were there? Thank you. I didn't know you were there. I saw you afterwards, but I didn't know you were in the room.

LEE: Yeah. Absolutely.

JOE: Well, part of the message, and it was a very simple message, was about three steps, and I want to reiterate them right here, because this is important to and relevant to the question.

I said that the universe, which you can call God, the Divine, the life energy, the life force (call it whatever it is to you; you know what I mean by this force that's bigger than all of us that we're all in, and that's wiser and stronger), whatever you want to call that (I'll call it Divinity), that Divinity is sending and receiving information and energy all the time. So that's the first thing to keep in mind. It is sending and receiving.

The second is that what it's sending and what it's receiving from you are being filtered through your belief system. This is very important. That energy coming in is very pure, but it hits you, and you have beliefs about what's possible for you. You have beliefs about the nature of reality. You have beliefs about your own worthiness. And the energy comes through, and gets filtered through your beliefs.

And then the third step is you get your results. And even when you look at your results, you filter your interpretation of them through your beliefs.

So if something doesn't happen as fast as you would like it to, most likely it's in the area of your beliefs.

I'm of the frame of mind that there's nothing impossible. I don't know, there may be things we haven't done yet, but my mind-set is there's nothing impossible. We may not know how to do it yet, but we can discover a way to do it, or invent a way to do it.

So if something's not happening, it could be hitting in a person's belief that's snagging it, and that belief could be something like "I don't really believe it's possible"; it could be "I don't really deserve this"; it could be something like "Well, this is going to cost me a lot of money when it actually arrives, so I'll have to pay taxes"; or whatever it happens to be.

And again, I'm making up beliefs. But I would invite everybody listening to be thinking about this, because if you stated that you want a particular result, and your sense is one of frustration, that's probably a signal that

you have beliefs that are causing it to not appear yet.
And I would suggest looking and playing with the idea
"If I really did have beliefs that would slow the manifestation process down, what might they be?" Something is going to surface, some sort of answer. It might
even seem crazy to you when it comes up.

When I was speaking on Sunday, I told people that
I was slowly increasing my income, and I had hit a
level at one point, and I couldn't seem to make any
more money than that particular level. All year long,
I just kind of leveled off. And I thought, "Well, why
is that? I have this clear intention. I believe that
Divinity is listening to me, and it's trying to help
me. I'm doing everything in my power, but I seem to
be hitting this roadblock. Why is it slowing down?
Why am I not getting more money?" And I looked at
my beliefs, and one of the beliefs that came up was
that I was not comfortable making more money than
my parents. And I remember when I said it on Sunday, you probably remember, the crowd kind of mur-
mured, like they all identified with it.

LEE: Right.

JOE: And I had to look at the belief. And I talked about it a
little bit on Sunday, saying, you know, our parents want
the best for us. They may not always know how to
express it, but they were doing the best they could.
And when I realized that, oh, my father would be proud
of me if I made more money than him, and when I
realized that I'd be able to help him, or anybody in my
family, or other people or other causes, as well as myself,
I was able to remove the barrier. And this is important.
The only barrier was my belief.

LEE: And would you say, Joe, that possibly those beliefs might not even appear to be related to the thing that you're wanting to achieve?

JOE: Yes. That's right.

LEE: Right? They could seem to be completely unrelated.

JOE: Well, you have an example, apparently, in your mind. What's coming up that might be useful to say?

LEE: Well, for example, I want to be successful at my business, and I want to grow my business.

JOE: Uh-huh.

LEE: And suppose it's not happening. But my limiting belief could be I'm not a likable person.

JOE: Oh, yeah, absolutely.

LEE: Right?

JOE: Absolutely.

LEE: And it has nothing to do directly with my business.

JOE: Oh, absolutely.

LEE: I'm selling real estate or I'm selling insurance.

JOE: Yeah.

LEE: But if I have a belief that I'm not likable as an individual, then obviously my customers aren't going to come to me.

JOE: Yeah, and that belief you may be totally unconscious of, until you start to do a call like this, or you get in the Miracles Coaching program and you work with somebody who can help you see it.

And I want everybody to realize I do this, too. You may look at me and say, oh, Joe has done all of this, and he has so many books, and you know, such and such career, and whatever level of success you perceive it to be. But I still have my limiting beliefs that surface. I still go forward, and I bump into something, and I still work with coaches, because I know that I am in a belief-driven universe, and most of those beliefs are unconscious.

You can question them on your own. I talked about it last Sunday. I'm giving you some methods on this call. But I often will turn to a coach, somebody outside of me, somebody who's objective, somebody who's not living the same belief system I am, so that I can become aware of those beliefs; and usually, once I become aware of them, just becoming aware of them often causes them to evaporate.

LEE: And actually, that takes us also to the next question, which I asked, which is why does it sometimes seem easier to attract negative things than positive things?

JOE: Yeah.

LEE: You know, what is it we're focusing on? Right?

JOE: Yup, it is that. In general, emotion is what's attracting everything into your life. Most people have intense hatred or anger or frustration. They attract more things that match that, because they're focused on that. If you can generate the same kind of emotion of love, or passion, for something that you really want, you will attract it instead.

My favorite example for me, and you'll probably laugh because I talked about all my cars on Sunday, too, but it was the idea that I've become this car fanatic, and I now love these cars. And it's ironic, because I work at home; I don't go to that many different places. When I do, I fly. So I have three beautiful cars, and don't drive any of them. And here I am feeling that I love them so much, they come into my life because I love them. They come

so easily because I love them. The love is what's attracting them.

So very often, people are more focused on what they
don't like, and they're generating a lot of energy for what
they don't like, and it's the energy that's going out there
attracting more to match it.

LEE: Why do some things manifest faster than others, when
I'm doing the same things for both? It seems like what
you just said would impact that. Say a little bit about
that.

JOE: Yeah. I think it goes back to the first part of the last two-
part question, where I was saying that we have beliefs
about it. So it may seem like it's working faster on one
than on the other, but I think if you look real closely,
you'll find that the only hindrance is some belief.

And of course, I don't know who the caller is, so I
don't know what the nature of their reality is, or what
their belief system is, but going back to my talk on
Sunday and this whole concept that Divine information
is coming to us, it's asking us to do things and sending
information to us. It's also sending information to us,
meaning when you state an intention, that's going
right into that zero state, right into the Divine, whatever
you want to call it. So it's going to bring the result to
you. This just seems to be the formula that works. The
only things that are going to slow it down, or absolutely
stop it, or even bring it to you, are your beliefs. So if it's
trying to come through, but for some reason you have a
limiting belief or a self-sabotaging belief, or a lack of
deservingness kind of thought, you will slow down the
process.

LEE: Okay. And I have one other question that's very similar, that I guess relates to limiting beliefs. Somebody wrote that it seems like each limiting belief uncovers another. Is there any end to them?

JOE: Well—

LEE: Sounds like someone wants an answer to all those limiting beliefs.

JOE: Yeah. Well, I guess I relate to that, and I want to say that you get to a place where there are none at all. And my experience has been that there are so many of them that they're just going to keep surfacing. But you don't have to buy into any of them. Once you've begun to do enough of this work, they shake off without you being attached to them. They'll surface, and you just let them go. It becomes almost a meditation, where the belief kind of comes across, like a thought coming across your mind right now, and you watch it like a cloud going through the sky. You're not the belief. You're not the thought. You're not the cloud. You are the one observing it. And I don't know if anybody is going to get this, because I still wrestle with this one, but if you could realize that you are the sky and not the clouds, you will be at total peace all the time.

LEE: Wow. I love that. That's great.

JOE: I'm going to repeat it, for me, if not for anybody else.

LEE: Yeah, please.

JOE: I'm going to say if you can realize you are the sky, not the clouds, you will be at peace all the time—the clouds being the thoughts that go by, the sky being the part of you that's observing them. If you can observe everything that's happening, you will be this detached, wonderfully at peace person who can be manifesting whatever you want.

LEE: Well, I think that's great, because it really leads me to the next question, this other question—

JOE: All right.

LEE: —which is, "What does it mean to be clear, and how do I know if I am clear?" So we talk with our clients a lot—

JOE: Yeah.

LEE: —in the mentoring program about being clear, and what you just said resonates for me—

JOE: Yeah.

LEE: —about that. Because that's what the sky is.

JOE: That's exactly what it is.

LEE: Uh-huh.

JOE: I say getting clear is the missing secret. And that was my talk last Sunday. I called it "The Missing Secret." It was all about getting clear.

I say getting clear is the missing secret to virtually every self-help program out there. You may find an exception or two, but across the board, they're not aware of this step, or they don't know how to handle this step. And what I'm referring to as being clear or getting clear means you don't have any beliefs in the way of achieving whatever your intention is. And you know you don't have any beliefs in the way because you easily manifest the thing that you want, or you're totally at peace while you know it's being manifested for you.

LEE: Aha. So there is a sense—

JOE: Yes.

LEE: —of peacefulness.

JOE: Yes.

LEE: Or a sense of nothing in the way.

JOE: Nothing in the way. If, for example, . . . you're trying to focus on health, or if you're trying to focus on wealth, or you're trying to focus on relationship, and you've declared your intention and you've done some belief work, but you feel a sense of frustration, you're not clear.

LEE: Right.

JOE: The sense of frustration is a signal that you still have a belief or two in the way. Or if you feel impatient, or if you feel a little angry, or if you feel any of these off-center, sad, grief-oriented, unhappy emotions, any of these emotions that you know aren't joyful, if you feel any of those emotions while going for your intention, it is a sign on the field, a red flag or a yellow flag, that you have a limiting belief or two. When you are clear, either you get your intention fulfilled pretty quickly or you know it's coming, and there's no sort of unpleasantness within you.

LEE: And I wondered, do you have your attention on it as much, either?

JOE: I don't think you do. I think that as long as it's playful, you can keep going back to your intention and saying wow, wouldn't it be great to have this particular relationship, or wouldn't it be great to have this much more money. As long as it's fun, you can revisit the intention. But if you keep revisiting because you think you have to, or you want to reinforce it, it may be hiding a belief that says you haven't done enough work or you don't believe the process is actually working. It could be a signal that there's a negative belief there.

LEE: So what I'm hearing you say, Joe, is that if I notice I'm upbeat, I'm playful, I'm excited about something, the likelihood that I'm clear—

JOE: Yes.

LEE: —is very good.

JOE: Absolutely.

LEE: Okay.

JOE: Those are key words. I often use the phrase *playful or childlike*. You know, if you walk by a store and you look inside and say wow, look at that guitar, it would be so much fun to be able to play that, but you're not needy about it, you're not desperate about it, you're not unhappy about it, you're not addicted to it, you're not attached to it, it's just a playful quality, you're not going to live or die because you have the guitar or not, but if you can look at it and say wow, it would be really cool to have it, you are probably in the most wonderful place to have that guitar within the next, you know, day or so.

LEE: Great. Okay. Good. So here's one other thing about not being clear. Somebody asked, "When I regularly notice I get upset with one person, and I suspect that there's a limiting belief, but I can't get to it, how do I figure it out?"

JOE: Yeah. That's a great question. Well, you know, I listened to Deepak Chopra speak Saturday night. And he's worth reading. He's a little harder to understand. He's Indian. He's a medical physician. He comes from a more, oh, historical background of ancient Hindu philosophy. But he was saying that, and I agree with this, there is nothing out there. Everything outside of yourself is an illusion, including other people.

LEE: Right.

JOE: And that it's all a mirror. It's all reflecting your own beliefs. And this is really powerful. It may be hard to accept the first time around, but—

LEE: Yeah.

JOE: —it's mind expanding and life transforming, when you really get it. And he was saying that if there are elements in another person that are really upsetting you, repulsing you, angering you, whatever it happens to be, most likely those are the same elements you have in you that you don't like. And that is so big to take on.

Deepak was talking about a woman who came up to him at a seminar, and she really pushed all of his buttons, and he felt like boy, this woman is rude, she's impatient, she's obnoxious. He had a whole list of things. And he thought later, "Wait a minute, I should take my own teachings to heart." So he wrote down all the elements that he saw in the other person he didn't like. Then he called his publicist and said, "I'm going to read a list of these traits to you, and I want you to tell me if I have these," and he listed them all, you know, like obnoxious, rude, and impatient. He went through the whole list, and he said the other side of the phone was dead quiet for a long time. And he thought oh, no. And he thought he'd better check it.

He then called his wife, and he read the same list to his wife, and then, he said, the silence on the other side of the phone was even longer this time than it was with his publicist. The point being those elements that he didn't like in the other person were the ones that he didn't like in himself. And so the belief clearing here is on you, not on another person. You can actually thank the other person, in person or in your own mind, as you make a list of the things you don't like, and then turn within to say, "Okay, how does this affect me? How is this part of my own personality that I haven't owned?"

LEE: That is so great, Joe, because what it reminds me of is Dr. Hew Len, and the ho'oponopono concept.

JOE: Exactly.

LEE: It's all about being responsible for everything that shows up in my life. So clearly, I have created this person in front of me so that I can deal with whatever it is in me—

JOE: Yeah.

LEE: —that is upsetting about them.

JOE: Yes, that's exactly it. And for those who are new on the call, and who don't know about Dr. Hew Len or the ho'oponopono—

LEE: That was my next question.

JOE: Okay. Well, there's a whole story behind it, and rather than tell the whole story, the shorthand version is this is a therapist at a mental hospital for the criminally insane, who helped heal an entire ward of patients, patients who had once had to be shackled or sedated because they were so dangerous, and he healed them using a Hawaiian technique called ho'oponopono. And I have learned this technique. I have met with Dr. Hew Len. We've done workshops together. We've coauthored a book called *Zero Limits*, and if you want to get a sense of what this is about, go to the web site www.ZeroLimits.info. It will tell you the story, and it will give you a sense of what he was doing that you can do today. But it's all the same. It's like there's nothing out there.

LEE: Right.

JOE: And this is very woo-wooish, in some ways, but for me, it's everyday reality. I have to look at everything that shows up in my life—and I don't care, good, bad, or indifferent—as a projection from the inside of me. And this goes back to my whole talk Sunday. The energy is coming into me, and as it goes through me, it's being filtered through my beliefs, and then I look out and I see the results. Well, those results aren't really real. What they are is a reflection of my beliefs. And if I don't like those results, I have to look at my beliefs. Change my belief, I get different results.

LEE: Wow. Okay. That's great. I have two more questions.

JOE: Okay.

LEE: One is, "I'm attracting everything I want—"

JOE: Good, good, good.

LEE: You like that.

JOE: Yes.

LEE: "—and I want those things for other people."

JOE: Yes.

LEE: "How do I have that happen for other people, especially those who are resistant—"

JOE: Yes.

LEE: "—to what I've learned?"

JOE: Okay. Well, there are two levels to this. I love the question. I love where that person is coming from, too, because that's the kind of noble caring about life and about the planet that I like to hear about.

LEE: Can I just tell you one thing, before you go further?

JOE: Sure.

LEE: I want you to know, almost every one of my clients has had that question.

JOE: Really.

LEE: They really have. You have the greatest customers.

JOE: That is so nice to hear.

LEE: They all want to know that.

JOE: That means their hearts are open. They want to change the world, not just themselves.

LEE: Yeah, that's true.

JOE: Well, the first part of this is we cannot violate another person's free will. We have to allow people to be wherever they're at. And believe me, I would love to change lots of people out there, but I've also got to remind myself of the second part of what I'm saying here. The second part of the statement is that they're a projection of me.

LEE: Right.

JOE: And so this goes back to the whole Dr. Hew Len method. You know, when Dr. Hew Len worked with those mentally ill patients, he didn't go to change any of them. He looked at their files, and he was repulsed because some of them were murderers or rapists, or, you know, they did very ugly things. And as he looked at their files, he saw that something would come up within him, and he did the ho'oponopono process within himself. As he did it within himself, they changed.

This is the whole point, that the whole world is within you. As you heal yourself, the outer world heals. You don't have to go and mess with other people. You don't have to be in their face. You don't have to think they're resistant. That's actually a

reflection of you. It's some part of your own resistance.

So, since I brought Dr. Hew Len up several times, let
me tell you what he did (to give you the shorthand
version here, and again, go to www.ZeroLimits.info to
read more). Dr. Hew Len basically would look within
himself and say to what I'll call the Divine (and again
this could be God, the universe, the life energy, the zero
state force, whatever you want to call that bigger
energy), he would be feeling whatever he's feeling
within himself, and say, "I love you," "I'm sorry," "Please
forgive me," and "Thank you"—those four phrases.
Consider it a mantra. Consider it a prayer. Call it
whatever you like—a poem—but he repeatedly said, "I
love you," "I'm sorry," "Please forgive me," and "Thank
you."

Now, he's not saying it to the other person. He's
not saying it out loud. He's not even looking at the
other person in most cases. He's saying it to the larger
force that we're all part of. He's saying it to the
greater energy. And he's not saying it to himself.
He's saying it silently, and he's saying it repeatedly:
"I love you," "I'm sorry," "Please forgive me," and
"Thank you." And what he's doing is trying to erase
those beliefs within him that help create what he's
seeing in the other person.

And as he's able to do it (this all goes back to belief
clearing, which is step two from my talk last Sunday),
as he's saying this, he's petitioning the Divine, saying,
"Look, I don't know where the beliefs came from. I'm
sorry for them; I love you; please forgive me for
whatever may have occurred to bring this into my

awareness; and thank you. Please forgive me, I love you, thank you. I'm sorry, please forgive me, thank you, and I love you." Just repeating those, and I change the order from time to time, you can do whatever you want. I think that if you just said "I love you" repeatedly you can just dilute any negativity that you might experience.

The point is you can't change other people. They have free will. But you work within yourself, and what you see on the other side, including people, is a projection anyway.

LEE: Yeah. That's great. That's great. Okay. And the last question I have is, "I heard the expression 'counter-intention.'"

JOE: Yes.

LEE: "What does that mean, and how do I know if I have them?"

JOE: Yeah. Well, I'm glad that one came up. I talked about that on Sunday, too, and I think we have it on the www.miraclescoaching.com web site. Occasionally I refer to it in my blog. And if you're not reading my blog, I encourage you to go do it, because I'm writing almost every day, and there are usually new insights, tips, and resources, and it's all free. Go to www.mrfire .com and on the left you'll see a link to my blog, and just go take a look.

So, counter-intentions. My favorite way of explaining this is think back to January 1st, New Year's Day. No doubt, you set some sort of resolution. You probably did it every year, and if you didn't do it this year, you've certainly done it in the past. New Year's resolutions could be: I'm going to go to the gym every day,

I'm going to stop overeating, I'm going to stop smoking, I'm going to, you know, date more. I don't know what it was, but you set some sort of New Year's resolution. You had the best of intentions. I've already talked about how powerful intentions are. You had the best of intentions to go to that gym. But on January 2nd or 3rd, you forgot where the gym was located.

So what happened? I say that you had a counter-intention. You had a hidden belief that was stronger than your intention. Your intention was: I'm going to get fit, I'm going to go to the gym. But that got pushed aside because of a hidden belief that I call a counter-intention that said I'm not going to go to the gym, I'm not going to go work out, I'm not going to get fit, for whatever reason.

These counter-intentions are what you want to get clear of. That's why I think Miracles Coaching is so powerful. That's why I use all these different techniques. That's why I still use a coach. That's why I think if we're going to move ahead in the world, we have to know what the counter-intentions are, which are limiting beliefs. They're the negativity.

Most of the time we don't know what they are, but with a little exploring and a little help, we can unearth them, shine the light on them, and let them go. If we want to move ahead in the world, those are the things we must release, because the only thing that, in my awareness, is stopping us from moving forward is us, and it's our beliefs. We are in a belief-driven universe. Change the beliefs, you get better results.

LEE: Change the beliefs and you get better results. I love that!

JOE: So do I! Godspeed to everyone listening. Go for your dreams!

---

Note: There are two DVDs of my presentation on "The Missing Secret" described at http://themissingsecret.info. These might be useful to you for further understanding the concepts presented in this book and mentioned in this teleseminar transcript.

# Five Insights on Manifesting Money
## Excerpts from a Miracles Coaching Teleseminar

I'm often asked about manifesting money. Here's what I tell people:

Money, all by itself, is nothing but paper and metal. It's coin and paperwork that we print this wonderful art on. Our money is so mystical, when you look at it. We've got "In God we trust," which, of course, few people notice and few people believe, and we also have a pyramid, which is very ancient and loaded with power and symbolism, with all kinds of possible interpretations in that symbol, and all kinds of ink used. I mean it's pretty amazing as a piece of art. But in and of itself, money is worthless. Money is nothing. Money is paper.

It's us who apply meaning to it. And that's where people start loading it with self-esteem issues, with control issues. We apply all kinds of meaning to the money.

And my advice is to start thinking of money like Monopoly money. It's fun. It's part of the game. But it does not determine whether you are happy or not happy, whether you are worthwhile or not worthwhile. It's got nothing to do with it.

I, personally, never go after money. I am never focused on money. I am focused on a passion, on fun, on sharing my heart, on doing good things, and maybe I might have one eye looking to see that I charge for what I'm doing, because it's so easy to just simply give it away, and I know that people don't value things if you don't put a price on them. A lot of marketing, for example, is perception, and a lot of perception is influenced by the price you put on something. But all of that is made up. Because the truth is that money, all by itself, is nothing. It's meaningless. It's paper. Whatever it means is what you make it mean.

So, again, from the Attractor Factor standpoint, you don't want to have feelings of need or attachment or addiction around money, because then you're sending out a feeling of need, attachment, and addiction, and it's going to cause an imbalance. You're going to be pushing money away. A part of you will be saying, "I want money, I want money, I want to do great things with money," and then another part of you is going to say, "I don't want money because money is evil, and rich people do bad things, and it will mean I'm greedy." And so a part of you is saying bring it on, and another part is saying keep it away, and what happens? You cancel it out, and you don't get any.

So part of my advice here, and this is such a big question that it really needs some coaching to get through it all, is to just look at money like Monopoly money. It's not a big deal. It's nothing, really. I mean certainly you can do things with it; it's a means of exchange, but it's because we've agreed on the meaning. It doesn't, by itself, have magical powers. You have the magical powers. So the focus needs to be on you, not on the money.

And if I had to give any more advice about the whole money thing, I would say to be focusing on what you love, because what everybody in the world wants is to love; they want to love and be loved. And if you can be focusing on sharing your heart with the people who most want to feel your heart, you'll end up receiving money. It will come as a by-product, as a side effect. It won't come as anything you're directly focused on.

And I know, at first glance, especially if you've heard this for the first time, you're going to think, "God, Joe's nuts. What is he talking about? It doesn't work like that." And I'm here to say it does work like that.

To give you another example, quite a while back, I took on a belief. Now, hear me out: I said I took on a belief. I consciously chose this belief, that the more money I spend, the more money I will receive. Now, that does not make any logical sense. If I tell it to an accountant, to a bookkeeper, to a banker, they're all going to say, "Ah, Joe, if you spend money, you will have less."

But I'm coming from a reinterpretation of how it works. And so I spend money, and as soon as I do, I start looking around, thinking, "Wow, I wonder where 10 times that amount is going to come from." So I'm more easily led to buying things and spending money, but because I have an expectancy that more is coming in because I'm spending money, it always comes in, and it overflows to the extent that I can create good causes and contribute money to them. I can help other people—I've helped my family, and I've helped friends. And of course, I can indulge in things like buying an expensive car when I already have cars and I work at home. I don't even drive anywhere.

So all of this is possible by letting money be neutral, and letting your self-esteem and your self-worth not be dependent on it. Let it be dependent on your satisfaction with yourself.

## Another Excerpt from a Miracles Coaching Teleseminar

The next question here is, "My intent seems to be all about finances. Is that okay? I have to say that other areas of my life are pretty much on the incredible side. Money is, and always has been, an issue for me."

Well, first of all, hey, it's fantastic that all of your life is pretty much on the incredible side. That's cool. Not everybody can say that. I think that is wonderful. Celebrate that, absolutely. Dance in the streets. Celebrate that most of your life is on the incredible side. Wow, what a wonderful statement to see, to hear, to live, to be the one to say.

So your intent is on finances. Is that okay? Absolutely. I don't think there's anything wrong with it. I think that money, again, is not evil. Money is not bad. People can use it, just like they can use any tool, for some sort of not very noble purpose. But I say that money itself, in and of itself, is totally fine. And if you want money, you want it for survival, you want it for the good that you can do with it, and you want it so you can spread it out to family and friends, I say it's all totally wonderful.

The way I look at the universe is what I said in the movie *The Secret*, in that one part where I said that the universe is like this great big catalog, and you just go through and pick out what you want. So if you want money, you can certainly go for money.

Now, again, my focus has never been on money. I certainly like money. Money comes into my life. I want it. I like it. I share it. It's a wonderful tool. It's wonderful to have money. That's an incredible thing to have. But it's not my focus. I don't think that's how it works, at least not for me. Maybe it does for other entrepreneurs, or people who make it into millions, or billionaires. I don't really know, in their cases.

I really believe that you have to have fun. I look at some of my heroes, who are making more money than me. Richard Branson, the famous tycoon and a billionaire, he says he's just having fun. He says yes to everything in life. He tries all kinds of things, and boy, he's having just a rocket ride of a good time.

And in fact, he's creating a rocket that's going to be sending people into space. And I think it costs $100,000 a seat. He's not doing it for the money. He's doing it because it's a challenge, and because it's fun. That's what his heart is directing him to do.

And then you look at Donald Trump. Donald Trump is a billionaire. And every time I read something about him, he never says he's trying to make money. He says, "I love deal making." And so he's expressing his love through deal making. He makes money as a result of it, and of course, he doesn't, sometimes. He went through debt and lost some property and did have some hard times for a while. But again, his focus was not on money. His focus was on doing what he thought was fun, which, in his case, was making deals.

In Richard Branson's case, it's doing anything that seems like it's a wild ride for him, and taking on challenges.

For me, it's whatever I get passionate about.

You know, I've just written a book on an ancient Hawaiian healing technique that I am absolutely enthralled by. It's called *Zero Limits*.

And *Zero Limits* is having the most profound effect on my life right now, more than just about anything I've done in the longest time, and so I've been putting my heart and soul into it. Of course, I've been busy with all kinds of other products and projects, and speaking and traveling and this, that, and the other, but that's been my focus.

And as I focus on my love and on my passion, finances just seem to get taken care of. So if you can take away your concern about finances (a Miracles Coach can help with that), and see where you're holding on to it, and just look at it in a nonjudgmental way, and focus more on the incredible life you've already got going, the more you can focus on your love, on your passion, and on your heart, the more likely some of those other concerns, like finances, will just disappear. They'll dissolve, and money will start to appear. And one day you'll look around, and you'll go, "I don't know where it's all coming from, but boy, I've got an incredible amount of money."

## Summary

Money, all by itself, is nothing but paper and metal. It's coin and paperwork that we print this wonderful art on. But in and of itself, money is worthless. It's us who apply meaning to it. And that's where people start loading it with self-esteem issues, with control issues. Whatever it means is what you make it mean. The focus needs to be on you, not on money.

My advice is to start thinking of money like Monopoly money. It's fun. It's part of the game. But it doesn't determine whether you are happy or not happy, whether you are worthwhile or not worthwhile. Money has nothing to do with it. Richard Branson, the famous tycoon and a billionaire, says he's just having fun. Donald Trump says, "I love deal making." His focus is on doing what he thinks is fun, which, in his case, is making deals.

I never go after money. I'm never focused on money. I'm focused on a passion, on fun, on sharing my heart, on doing good things, and maybe I might have one eye looking to see that I charge for what I'm doing, because it's so easy to just simply give it away, and I know that people don't value things if you don't put a price on them.

From the Attractor Factor standpoint, you don't want to have feelings of need or attachment or addiction around money, because then you're sending out a feeling of need, attachment, and addiction, and it's going to cause an imbalance. You're going to be pushing money away.

Focus on what you love, because what everybody in the world wants is to love; they want to love and be loved. And if you can be focusing on sharing your heart with the people who most want to feel your heart, you'll end up receiving money. It will come as a by-product, as a side effect. It won't come as anything you're directly focused on.

So all of this is possible by letting money be neutral, and letting your self-esteem and your self-worth not be dependent on it. Let it be dependent on your satisfaction with yourself.

As I focus on my love and on my passion, finances just seem to get taken care of.

If you can take away your concern about money (and again, a Miracles Coach can help you with that), and see where you're holding on to it, and just look at it in a nonjudgmental way, and focus more on the incredible life you already have, then other concerns, like finances, will just disappear, and money will start to appear. And one day you'll look around, and you'll say, "I don't know where it's all coming from, but boy, I've got an incredible amount of money."

# What Is Miracles Coaching?

*If you really believe in your I Amness, you must test yourself by daring to assume you are now the being you desire to be.*

—Neville Goddard

About 15 years ago I made a promise: Whenever I noticed I wasn't clear, I would instantly do something about it. I would reach for one of the clearing methods you've learned in this book. Usually, that was enough. But I admit that there were times when I felt like I was stuck in the quicksand of my own mind. At those times, I would call for help.

Over the years I've developed relationships with people I now call Miracles Coaches. Because I knew this worked for me, I set up a program where others could have a Miracles Coach, too.

As you know, I've experienced the difference that being clear can make. In the past, when I thought about having my dream life—the one where miracles happen every day—I stopped myself. Who was I kidding? How could that be possible? I was living on the streets!

Well, I know now—and you know—that miracles can and do happen. And I know that being clear is the key to getting there. There is a real challenge in this for some of you. Actually, it is three challenges: *knowing* the ways to get clear, *being* clear, and *staying* clear.

That's what this book is about. In it, I've shared with you 10 methods I know to get clear and stay that way.

But there is one more thing I've seen that can really make a difference in getting clear. Like lots of other things in life, getting and staying clear will be lot easier for some of you when you have a little help.

That help is called Miracles Coaching, and it's all about having a partner in the getting clear process.

Lots of people come to me with questions about getting clear and staying clear and how I successfully do that on a day-to-day basis. I have to say that having a Miracles Coach has been the one thing that made the major difference for me.

That's because the principal benefit of getting or staying clear is that it allows you to be present in the moment, with nothing in the way. I found, though, that many times old memories or past beliefs about myself just kept popping up, no matter what I did.

Sometimes, I didn't even know that's what was in the way. It just seemed that I never got what I wanted—and all I could ever think about was how to get rid of what I didn't want or what I should or shouldn't have done. Sound familiar?

Well, with a coach, I found it so much easier to clear out those past memories and limiting beliefs that were keeping me stuck. That's why I created the Miracles Coaching program.

Miracles Coaching is a unique way to take on the process of clearing those beliefs. Someone is there to help you see them; that's what makes the difference. An outside mind can see something that to you is invisible—until you talk with your coach.

## How Does Miracles Coaching Work?

People often say to me, "Joe, I know Miracles Coaching works, but *how* does it work? What makes it so effective?" There are four parts to Miracles Coaching that make it so powerful:

1. The program design and structure.
2. The Miracles Coaching methodology.
3. The coaching expertise.
4. The personalized nature of the program.

Let's look into each of these parts, which work synergistically, to help you go beyond what you may be able to accomplish on your own.

### Program Design and Structure

The structure we've set up for the program allows for a strong foundation for miracles:

*Time:* Typically, sessions are held weekly for three to six months. This time frame works well for those deeply rooted limiting beliefs to surface and be cleared and for you to deepen your understanding of the Laws of Attraction. In addition, your coach is available through e-mail and for just-in-time coaching between sessions.

*Fieldwork:* Exercises and study materials between sessions comprise a key piece of the Miracles Coaching program success, as this is where miracles show up—on the court of life. It's by doing these exercises that clients really take on the kind of exploratory conversations that engage their hearts and minds. This gives them the ability to alter old ways of thinking and encourages awareness of new possibilities for their future. People often say about the fieldwork, "This alone was worth the cost of the program." That's how powerful it is!

*Feedback:* It is valuable to have access to feedback as you practice what you are learning in the Miracles Coaching program. Sometimes just getting confirmation that you are on the right track is all you need to remove the doubt and take action.

*Commitment and Accountability:* When I designed this program, I discovered that part of the process of creating miracles is being accountable for your greatness!

The Miracles Coaching program holds you to account for that greatness, even when you don't. Right up front, in the foundational agreements both you and your coach make, as well as in the promises made during the program, your coach holds you (lovingly, of course) to account.

Another piece in that equation is the Miracles Coaches' commitment to your success. That's what has them willing to talk with you about subjects that might, under other circumstances, be uncomfortable to confront. This level of commitment—the willingness to not step over anything—is one of the greatest gifts the Miracles Coach can give.

When someone is willing to face the uncomfortable stuff and talk to me about things that might be tough to deal with, I know I've got a real partner.

*Program Design:* The great thing about this program is that each session builds on earlier sessions, so it gives you more than intellectual understanding. You can get the physical, practical experience that comes when you clear those limiting beliefs. I notice that when it happens, I actually feel lighter! And it's that lightness and clarity that make creating miracles real in your life.

The depth and breadth of the program design are pretty amazing in that the program allows beginners *and* folks who've been studying the Law of Attraction for quite a while to grow and gain mastery of clearing the stuff that keeps them stuck.

### There's a Method to the Madness

When I created the program, I drew from a number of different sources: *The Attractor Factor, The Secret, Zero Limits,* and manifestation secrets I haven't even published—yet! I believe that it's this broad variety of methods that is responsible for the amazing effectiveness of the program. It has been tried, tested, and finally demonstrated by our clients that the Miracles Coaching methodology fulfills its promise to create miracles.

### Expertise of the Coach

Miracles Coaches are senior coaches who come from a wide variety of coaching and spiritual backgrounds. Each has been trained and certified by me. Their expertise is what allows people to make such fast progress.

### Personalized Nature of the Program

Do you remember the television show called *This Is Your Life?* People would come and talk about someone and how much the person did for them and why the person should be rewarded for it. Well, in this case, this is *your* life and these are *your* miracles and you deserve the rewards that miracles can bring!

Your Miracles Coach is there to support you in having that miraculous life. He or she will take into account where you are in your development, what you want to accomplish, other training you've had, your personal style of learning, and other factors to make sure this is truly *your* program.

For example, information could be delivered either in a different order or to a different level of depth, depending on your needs. And your coach may emphasize some principles or distinctions in your program that another client isn't ready for or hasn't any interest in.

All of these factors—the structure, the methodology, the expertise, and the personalization, plus the dedication of the Miracles Coaches—help this program produce results.

## So, Who Is a Miracles Coach?

When I'm asked this question, here's what I say is important to know. When I worked with a coach, it was important to me that he or she be intelligent, have compassion, care deeply for others, and have a broad background in a wide variety of subjects. That's why the Miracles Coaches I certify come from many disciplines and have arrived at Miracles Coaching through many paths. They are writers, artists, and business experts; they are management, marketing, and training gurus. And they are all individuals committed to contributing their lifelong learning gifts to others.

I've found, over time, that the Miracles Coach's mastery of living a miraculous life, combined with a client's commitment to produce results, provides the kind of environment that creates clarity and the possibility for amazing, miraculous things to happen.

If you're up to creating miracles and want a partner to help you clear out the past and create a miraculous future, check out Miracles Coaching.

For more information, see www.miraclescoaching.com.

# Bonus: Emotional Freedom 101

## Letting Go of Unwanted Thoughts or Feelings

### Peter Michel

*www.emotionalfreedom101.com*

## What Are Feelings?

Feelings are programs (like computer programs) put in by the mind as being *pro*-survival. However, they are all, in fact, *anti*-survival, as they are programs based in the past and they keep us acting/reacting from the past conditioning, instead of being able to respond in the moment. They impair our responsibility—our ability to respond and to discriminate. When our feelings are intense, we could be sitting on railroad tracks with a train heading right for us, and we could actually miss seeing it. Our feelings can take us over completely. Often they unconsciously *run us* instead of us *running them*. All these programs stem from one place: *desire*, a feeling of *lack*.

## Where Are Feelings?

Feelings are of the mind, yet they show up in our body as energy sensations. The body is an extension (or condensation) of our mind and habitual thinking. Nothing can appear in the body unless a thought of it was held in the mind sometime prior. It is much like the body we create in a night dream. It appears so real in a night dream, yet when we awaken, we realize that our body in our dream was really only in our mind. The same is true in this daydream, which, to too many of us, often becomes more like a "day-mare" due to mismanaged emotions.

The body is like a computer printout of the mind. Thus, we can recognize our state of mind by how our body feels. Is it tense or relaxed? Does it feel good or bad? Is there fear and clutching in the stomach or chest, or is there faith of mind and heart and ease in the body? Are we breathing short, tight, shallow breaths, or are we breathing long, slow, deeply relaxed diaphragmatic breaths?

## Whose Feelings Are They?

Do your feelings belong to your parents? To your neighbor? To your child or spouse? Whose feelings are they that you experience in your body? They are *yours*, of course. This is a very good thing. It means that if you don't like them, you can do something about them.

## Why Release Feelings?

Presumably, you want to be happy. You want to feel free. You want to be abundant and at peace.

Letting go of the built-up negative feelings will quiet the mind, eliminate self-sabotage programming, draw abundance toward us effortlessly, and bring us a happiness that never leaves us.

In any moment either we are suppressing and building up our lacking, limiting feelings like computer viruses or we are releasing and discharging them from our body-mind system, allowing the body-mind to function flawlessly like a super-computer. The choice is always ours in every moment.

Almost all illness is stress-related. All lack comes from lacking, limiting feelings in the body-mind. Destructive relationships come from negative, nonlove feelings being suppressed and then later expressed toward our friends, family, and partners.

So, which would you rather do? Build them up and experience more lack, illness, and disharmony? Or release them and experience more abundance, health, and love?

## When Can I Release My Unwanted Feelings?

There is only one moment in time where we can deal with our feelings: *now.*

Even though our mind may jump backward and forward in what we call time, we can access and deal with our feelings only in the present moment. When we are here now, we can deal with our feelings as *energy.*

We may think to ourselves, "I'll address these feelings later," yet how many times does "later" never come? So why not let go of your feelings now, in the moment you feel them, instead of carrying them around with you?

## What about Positive Feelings? Why Would I Want to Let Those Go?

There are no positive or negative feelings. There is only emotional energy (e-motion = energy in motion) that gets labeled as positive or negative.

But, for the sake of this book, let us assume that there are positive and negative feelings.

When you release any negative feelings, you are left freer, lighter, and happier as those feelings *leave.*

When you release any positive feelings, you are left freer, lighter, and happier as those positive feelings *increase.*

So, when you perform emotional releasing on both the positive and negative feelings . . .

The negative feelings drop.

The positive feelings increase.

Good deal, huh?

What is really happening is you are simply removing the covering over your true self, which is happiness itself.

Feelings cover over our true nature and obscure it. They keep us constantly looking away from the perfect, whole, and complete being that we always are.

Thoughts and feelings are ever changing. They are in the realm of phenomena. They come and they go like the weather. Releasing gets you *beyond* the limited phenomenon into the realm of the neumenon, which is the ground state of being, sometimes referred to as witness consciousness. This is the pure "I" of us we refer to when we say to someone, "I am . . . ," when we talk about ourselves.

Have you ever wondered, who are you as this pure "I" when it is not attached to a label or associated with other things? This is the pure core that is ever untouched, unchanged, undisturbed, unaltered, ever happy, ever peaceful, and ever free. It is the being that we *are*.

Lester Levenson said, "The easiest way to contact the Self (God) is through the feelingness in the heart of 'I,' or 'I Am,' with nothing more added. This feelingness is the Self, the Real—Inner Self. The moment we add anything at all, like 'I am good or bad'; 'I am poor or rich'; 'I am great or small'; or 'I am that'; we are imposing a limitation on the 'I Am' and creating the ego."

All of the positive feelings are actually our very own being-ness, which we are tasting when we let go of the covering (feelings) over it. When we drop our emotions, the mind quiets and this innate sense of self (happiness) becomes self-obvious to us. However, often we attribute this happiness to some other person, place, or thing that we think "made us happy." What actually happened was that a desire got satisfied, and when it did, the mind went quiet and we tasted the "yummyness" of our very own being. We then figured it was the thing or person or achievement that gave us this feeling: "I am so happy to be in love with him (or her)." "All this money has made me so happy." "I am so happy I got this new car (or job, or award, or fame, and so on)." This is never the case.

A quick story that highlights this is a story about the dog that came across a bone. He thought to himself, "Yum, a juicy bone!" He took it in his jaws, chomped down on it, and it shattered into razor-sharp shards in his mouth. It was a dry bone! These shards cut his gums and they bled. As his mouth bled, he tasted his own blood and attributed it to the bone, thinking, "Wow, this sure is a juicy bone. But it sure does hurt!" He then proceeded to bite down harder, taste more of his own blood, feel more pain, and continue to attribute the tastiness to the bone. Sound familiar?

What we are really after is our own "blood," our pure, silent consciousness (awareness) beyond identification with limited thought, feeling, and form. When we are in a silent space of beingness, there are no feelings. The feelings arise only when we return to the mind and think to ourselves, "Wow, that felt great (to be without all that painful thinking)!" The mind can never comprehend the peace of our true self. Its job is to always identify a certain state ("I feel happy," "I feel sad," etc.). It labels and judges. The moment we label and judge, we are no longer in the now experiencing. We are into thinking about the experience. This is like looking at a picture of a strawberry instead of biting into it and tasting its sweet juiciness.

## What Do Feelings Feel Like?

Feelings can take the form of many bodily sensations, including:

- Energy
- Heat
- Tingling
- Pressure
- Waves
- Itching
- Pain
- Yawning (moving energy)
- Tension
- Tightness/Contraction
- Clutching
- A knot
- Lightness
- Heaviness
- Numbness

## How Do I Release My Feelings?

There are many different ways to release an unwanted thought or feeling. This report explores 17 of them. There are many more.

## What Is the Best and Fastest Way to Do Emotional Clearing?

There is a technique called the Release® Technique, which is taught in a course called the Abundance Course.®

It is given through an experiential training that is taught either via a live class, in a home study course on CDs, or through a book. I do not, however, recommend learning this technique from a book, as if you get it as mere head knowledge you can't expect it to benefit you very much. The guidance of a trained teacher is crucial for getting the most from it. However, a book can be a great reference after one learns the technique through a live class or audio lessons that guide one—repeatedly—in strengthening the "releasing muscle" and ability to let go of unwanted feelings instantly.

Most of the techniques covered in this report are *not* part of the *Abundance Course*, though they have all been tested to be very effective for releasing stuck and unwanted emotions that cause needless suffering and cloud our discrimination.

The techniques are approaches that I either have personally discovered or have gathered in my years of exploring emotions and our ability to let them go at will. I attempt to always give credit where credit is due. However, there may be some techniques I learned many years ago where I do not recall the person who first taught them to me. In such a case, please accept my apologies if proper attribution is not given and know that your contribution to the field of emotional releasing is much appreciated.

The specific style of releasing is not very important. What is important is practicality. How well do they work?

Do they simply release emotions one by one, or do they strike the root generators of all negativity, lack, and limitation? The *Release* Technique strikes the root. It is the only technique I have found that allows people to identify these root generators as they operate and guides them in dumping them fast without any story or trying to figure them out.

## Why Strike the Root Generators of Feelings?

If you don't strike the root generators of feelings, you'll constantly be regenerating more and more negativity, lack, and limitation. When you strike the root cause of the emotions, you will quiet the mind much faster than they will be able to regenerate. Eventually, you are left with a totally quiet mind.

How quiet? I describe it as the peace of being on a quiet street corner in the middle of nowhere at 3 AM surrounded by freshly fallen snow. All is calm; all is bright. This is the natural state of pure awareness, which comes when the mind quiets.

Here's an example of striking the root generators:

Have you ever seen those plates on the spring-loaded racks in some cafeterias? You take one plate off and the next one pops up; you take that off and the next one pops up, and so on and so forth. Well, our feelings are like that, only there's no end to the plates (feelings) if the generators are still in place. However, if you release the root generators, it's like removing stacks of plates at a time, and you get to that place of inner peace and quiet much faster and your feelings stop regenerating so quickly.

## How to Get the Most Out of This Report

When you notice a problem or an unwanted thought or feeling, review the list of 17 techniques for the step-by-step releasing exercise that feels right for you in the moment.

This list is a virtual toolbox of ways to release. It is not meant to be a be-all and end-all guide to letting go, but it offers some wonderful and varied approaches to letting go.

Not everyone releases in the same way. Sometimes the ego-mind is resistant to one approach, but then another approach will assist it in letting go of the negative feelings (anti-survival programs). It holds them because it thinks it is protecting us. But if you look at how many times your destructive emotions have sabotaged your life, health, finances, and relationships, you'll quickly realize it hasn't done such a great job. Instead, through fear and negativity, it has kept you focusing on what you do *not* want in life, thus causing you to attract more of what you don't want. These techniques reverse that tendency, allowing you to release the negative emotions and thus focus on and attract more of what you *do* want.

## Releasing Q&A

Q: *How can I know if I'm truly releasing?*

A: Measure it. Before you start releasing, it is often helpful to measure the intensity of the feeling on a scale of 0 to 10, with 0 being calm and released and 10 being extremely intense and undesirable. Then, after you go through the releasing steps, rate it again on this scale and you should notice it has been noticeably reduced.

Doing this before and after releasing adds validation that you are actually releasing the feelings. This is important, as the mind will try to keep us holding on to them and will often trick us into thinking that nothing is happening or we aren't getting anywhere, so that we give up. This scale will at least give us a bit more clarity in terms of any shift occurring in our subjective degree of emotional intensity.

Q: *I feel stuck. Now what?*

A: Let go of wanting to change or get rid of the stuck feeling. It will move.

Q: *I don't feel anything. How can I release what I can't feel?*

A: You can't. You need to first feel the feeling in order to let it go. You don't have to feel the full charge or intensity of it, but you need to bring some of it up into your conscious awareness.

Often we have suppressed our feelings for so long and have lived in our heads so much that we have forgotten what it feels like to feel. Thus, we are often very suppressed at first. This is resistance that covers over and protects the other feelings. Simply welcome any blank or numb feelings. These are feelings, too. Notice them and let go of wanting to change them. They will move and will reveal deeper feelings beneath them that are being suppressed. Once those feelings come up, apply steps to release them as described in this report.

Q: *What if I have a mental or emotional condition that I am being treated by a therapist for?*

A: This is not a substitute for therapy, but it can often work as a very powerful adjunct. Please consult your therapist before doing any of these exercises. Some of them can allow a great deal of emotional energy to come up, and this can seem overwhelming if your emotional state is already challenged. If you're on medications, ask your doctor if he or she can reduce them, as they will often suppress the feelings, which does not help when you're trying to allow them up to be released and resolved.

Q: *When I release a feeling, a deeper feeling seems to come up.*

A: Our feelings are often suppressed in layers, like an onion. Often we peel away one layer and there's a deeper layer beneath it. Just keep going, and you'll get lighter and lighter. The fastest way to cut through all the layers is through the Release Technique, which teaches you how to strike the root of all the layers, which clears large chunks of emotions with ease.

## The Techniques

Are you ready?

Let's get started.

For each approach, I'll give you a step-by-step example for clarity. Some of these are repetitious, but the repetition is to get you used to the basic process of really tuning in to the actual energy or sensation of the feeling, instead of merely thinking about it or labeling it intellectually.

## Emotional Freedom 101: 17 Ways to Release Any Unwanted Thought or Feeling on the Spot

### 1. Welcome the Feeling

Welcoming a feeling is the opposite of resisting it.

Welcoming dissolves the resistance that normally keeps feelings suppressed and stuck.

Here's a simple how-to on welcoming your feelings:

1. Put your head down and place your hand on your stomach or chest to assist you in *feeling* the sensation of the feeling.
2. Notice the feeling in your body.
3. Rate the feeling on a scale from 0 to 10.
4. Assume an attitude of welcoming the feeling, just as you would welcome a friend in through the front door of your house. Just open up to the feeling and let it come in, inviting it into your awareness in a greater way and welcoming it into your consciousness instead of looking away from it and avoiding the sensation of it.
5. As you welcome the feeling that was previously unwanted, you will find that it lessens or dissolves (because you stopped resisting it).

6. Rate the feeling again on the scale from 0 to 10. Did it lessen? If so, you are heading in the right direction. Keep going until it is zero. If it is not lessening, go back through the steps or try another approach.

## 2. Dive into Your Feeling

When you dive into the core of any feeling, one of two things will happen:

If it's a negative feeling such as anger, grief, or fear, it will dissolve, usually instantly.

If it's a positive feeling such as peace, love, or gratitude, it will increase.

This exercise is similar to welcoming the feeling, yet a little different:

1. Put your head down and place your hand on your stomach or chest to assist you in *feeling* the sensation of the feeling.
2. Notice the feeling in your body.
3. Rate the feeling on a scale from 0 to 10.
4. Noticing the sensation of the feeling in the body, allow yourself to dive into the sensation of it. That is, bring your awareness into the core of it and see what's there.
5. What's in the middle of the feeling? What does it *feel* like?
6. If you truly dove into it with feeling instead of just thinking about it, you will notice it began lessening or evaporating (or is gone completely), as there is literally nothing holding the feeling together. It is held there by only one thing: resistance to it. When we look for the core of the feeling, we are making the feeling conscious, and consciousness dissolves feelings.
7. Rate the feeling again on the scale from 0 to 10. Is it less? If so, you are heading in the right direction. Keep going

until it is zero. If it is not lessening, go back through the steps or try another approach.

When we are 100 percent nonresistant to our feelings, they pass through effortlessly and we remain wide open and free.

### 3. Increase It Mentally (Double It)

Why would you want to mentally increase or double the intensity of a feeling?

You've got it: Because doing so dissolves it.

I once worked in a holistic health clinic, the largest on the East Coast. The director of the clinic, who was an acupuncturist and doctor of oriental medicine, once told me that the way to get rid of a charley horse cramp in your leg is to "grab it and squeeze the dickens out of it." He explained that if you have a yang state (tension) and you apply more yang (more tension), it will flip around into a yin state (released). I tried this, and it actually worked. And it works very well with feelings, too! It's the same principle.

Here's how to apply it to your feelings:

1. Put your head down and place your hand on your stomach or chest to assist you in *feeling* the sensation of the feeling.
2. Notice the feeling in your body.
3. Rate the feeling on a scale from 0 to 10.
4. Now, allow it to increase or double in intensity.
5. Mentally increase the sensation of the feeling more, and more, and more.
6. As you increase it, you will notice it will lessen or dissolve.
7. Rate the feeling again on the scale from 0 to 10. Is it less? If so, you are heading in the right direction. Keep going

until it is zero. If it is not lessening, go back through the steps or try another approach.

This technique works for two reasons:

1. According to quantum physics, you cannot have two things occupying the same space at the same time. When you try to have the feeling and *more* of the feeling in the same place at the same time, they cancel each other out and dissolve.
2. Nonresistance dissolves. As you are allowing the feeling to increase, you are no longer resisting it, which allows it to come up, pass through, and dissolve without effort.

## 4. Let Go of Wanting It to Go Away

Usually, when we don't like a feeling or a thought, we fight with it. We resist it and want it to go away. This effectively allows us to hold on to it.

When you let go of wanting to change, control, or get rid of any unwanted feeling, stuck or numb sensation, or resistance, you allow it to change and dissolve—leaving greater freedom and expansiveness. Letting go of the "wanting to change" energy allows any stuck or numb energy to move.

1. Put your head down and place your hand on your stomach or chest to assist you in *feeling* the sensation of the feeling.
2. Notice the feeling in your body.
3. Rate the feeling on a scale from 0 to 10.
4. Notice how you don't like the feeling and how you want to get rid of it.
5. Allow yourself to let go of wanting to change it or get rid of it, just for right now.

6. You'll notice it will have immediately reduced in intensity or shifted completely.

7. Rate the feeling again on the scale from 0 to 10. Is it less? If so, you are heading in the right direction. Keep going until it is zero. If it is not lessening, go back through the steps or try another approach.

Wanting to change or control it is holding in mind "lacking change," so it stays stuck.

Letting go of wanting to change any thought or feeling allows it to move.

5. Feel Love

1. Put your head down and place your hand on your stomach or chest to assist you in *feeling* the sensation of the feeling.

2. Notice the feeling in your body.

3. Rate the feeling on a scale from 0 to 10.

4. Notice any nonlove feelings you may be holding toward your feelings.

5. Make a decision to feel love for whatever you are feeling.

6. Feel love for yourself and your feeling:

    1. Say "I love you" to the feeling.

    2. Allow yourself to feel love for your feeling.

    3. Then, feel love for yourself as you feel your feeling.

7. Say "Yes" to (accept/approve of) whatever thought or feeling arises.

8. Rate the feeling again on the scale from 0 to 10. Is it less? If so, you are heading in the right direction. Keep going until it is zero. If it is not lessening, go back through the steps or try another approach.

The four aspects of love are allowing, acceptance, approval, and appreciation. Choose one (or more) of these aspects and feel that for your feelings.

Resistance is the universal "icer" for our feelings. It freezes them.

Allowing, accepting, approving, and appreciating melt the frozen feelings and allow them to flow and the energy to move.

Love is the universal deicer that dissolves hardened, stuck, and limiting feelings like a hot knife slices through butter.

This exercise will allow you to reclaim any energy you have unconsciously invested in your feelings when you resisted or fought with them.

### 6. Appreciate Unwanted Feelings Away

This is very similar to the previous exercise, only the focus here is on appreciation and gratitude for the feeling:

1. Put your head down and place your hand on your stomach or chest to assist you in *feeling* the sensation of the feeling.
2. Notice the feeling in your body.
3. Rate the feeling on a scale from 0 to 10.
4. Feel gratitude for the thought or feeling and say "Thank you" to it.
   - Why be grateful for it? Because that negative thought or feeling is there because on some level you feel it is serving you in some way—perhaps to keep you safe somehow. However, only positive feelings can keep us safe. Negative feelings pull more negativity into us. So, feeling gratitude for the feeling pulls you up into positivity, and you can't feel blessed and stressed at the same time.
   - You can't be in gratitude and negativity at the same time. Thus the negativity must dissolve.

5. Rate the feeling again on the scale from 0 to 10. Is it less? If so, you are heading in the right direction. Keep going until it is zero. If it is not lessening, go back through the steps or try another approach.

## 7. Just Drop the Feeling

This is one of the simplest and fastest ways to release any unwanted thought or feeling.

Try this:

1. Grab a pen.
2. Clutch it in your hand.
3. Clutch it tightly and hold it to your stomach or chest or where you usually notice you're holding on to your emotions.
4. Feel the tension of your hand gripping and grasping the pen until it's almost uncomfortable.
5. That's how we hold on to our feelings.
6. Now, extend your arm out in front of you, still gripping the pen, and turn your palm toward the floor.
7. Now, relax your fingers and allow the pen to drop.
8. See how easy that was? That's how easy it is to drop *any* unwanted thought or feeling on the spot.

Feelings never hold us. We, in fact, hold them. The feelings want to flow as energy. It is us who restrict them by grasping them. So, let them flow and let them go!

## 8. Do Conscious Comparisons

We would never knowingly hurt or limit ourselves; however, unconsciously, we do so every single day.

By making the unconscious conscious, we discriminate (we see what we're doing), and in this seeing we tend to spontaneously release that which does not serve us.

It is actually discrimination that makes releasing possible. Doing conscious comparisons shows us that we are not our feelings, that our feelings are not holding us, and that we have a choice to hold on to the feelings or let them go.

Here's a series of questions you can ask yourself to open up your discrimination. This is a mindful exercise that uses the mind to undo its limitations.

After you ask each question, ask yourself which you will choose for yourself in this moment.

1. When I think about _____ (insert problem or situation causing stress), do I feel positive or negative? *Consciously choose to be positive.*
2. Am I free or bound? *Which do you choose?*
3. Is this love or fear? *Which do you choose?*
4. Is this doubt or faith? *Which do you choose?*
5. Is this abundance or lack? *Which do you choose?*
6. Is this oneness or separation? *Which do you choose?*
7. Is this peace or disturbance (fear)? *Which do you choose?*
8. Is this release/ease or contraction? *Which do you choose?*
9. Am I one with this person/feeling/problem or separate? *Which do you choose?*
10. Am I saying "Yes" or "No" to _____ (abundance, myself, freedom, my goal, etc.)? *Which do you choose?*
11. Am I welcoming or rejecting? *Which do you choose?*
12. Am I open or closed? *Which do you choose?*
13. Am I relaxed or contracted? *Which do you choose?*
14. Would I rather be free or bound? Happy or unhappy? Peaceful or afraid? Secure or insecure? *Which do you choose?*
15. Am I pushing or grasping, or am I accepting and letting things be as they are? *Which do you choose?*

16. Am I giving to others and to life, or am I desiring/wanting from them? *Which do you choose?*
17. Am I noisy or quiet inside? *Which do you choose?*

## 9. Be as the Sky

Nature can remind us of *our* true nature.

1. Look up into the sky.
2. Do you notice any clouds floating through it, or is it simply open and expansive?
3. Notice how the sky neither grabs hold of clouds (or birds, or airplanes, or satellites, etc.), nor does it try to push them away. It neither allows them nor rejects anything. The sky simply is as it is—open space.
4. Feel the expansiveness and openness of the sky.
5. Notice what this openness awakens in you—a deeper, wider, more expansive state of awareness.
6. If any thoughts or feelings arise, simply watch them as they pass through like clouds. Witness them without attachment or wanting to get rid of them. Just let them pass through.
7. Keep returning to the feeling of openness within you that is the same as the openness of the sky.

You cannot see anything outside of you that is not within you. Thus, the limitlessness of sky and space that you see is in you as well.

## 10. Float It Away

Our minds often pull us into thought streams like rushing rivers.

We don't have to go with them.

The next time you notice yourself being pulled into unwanted thoughts or feelings, try this:

1. In your mind's eye, kneel beside a rushing river, safely on the dry bank.
2. Feel the rush of your feelings within you.
3. Place those feelings into the rushing river.
4. Allow them to be quickly swept away.
5. Allow any thoughts, feelings, or concerns to rush to the ocean and dissolve into its vastness like salt.
6. Bring your awareness back to your still, silent self, sitting quietly on the bank, free of the disturbing emotions.
7. If there are any more emotions, keep dropping them into the rushing river, allowing them to be swept into the ocean until you are completely quiet inside.

## 11. Let Go of Disapproving of Yourself or Your Feeling

Most of us are disapproving of ourselves and our feelings constantly.

This is like having a broken leg and beating it with a stick. It doesn't help it! It hurts it and makes it worse.

When you feel an unwanted feeling, do this:

1. Look for the disapproval energy.
2. Welcome it up.
3. Allow yourself to begin letting go of any disapproving energy toward yourself or your feeling or thought.
4. Do this more . . . and more . . . and more . . . until it is gone.
5. Take time each day to notice any disapproval and choose to let it go until it is gone.

Trying to move forward and feel love while disapproving of ourselves is like trying to drive with the brakes on. It is impossible to feel love when we are disapproving of ourselves, and it is usually totally habitual for most of us.

After letting go of the disapproval energy, you will feel free to move into *approval* energy more fully.

## 12. Give Yourself Approval

Give yourself unconditional approval—just because you're breathing and you're alive!

What does it mean to give yourself approval? It means to like or accept yourself.

If you find this difficult, go back to the previous exercise and let go of more disapproval; otherwise, you are "driving with the brakes on."

Here's an incremental approach I learned from Kam Bahkshi, a Release Technique graduate:

1. Start with a thimbleful of approval—just a little bit. Pour it over your head and let it soak in.
2. Once you've taken that in, give yourself even more—an egg cup full. Receive it.
3. Then give yourself even more—a coffee mug full.
4. And then, even more—a bucketful.
5. And even more—a bathtub full.
6. And even more—a waterfall of approval energy.
7. Then a lake of positive, loving, self-approval energy.
8. And finally, an entire ocean of approval.
9. Allow yourself to float like a sponge in this ocean of pure positive acceptance and approval.
10. Allow it to soak in and saturate every cell. Just marinate in it.

You may want to memorize this entire progression and do it daily with your eyes shut. This is a very powerful exercise for health, happiness, abundance, and freedom.

## 13. Float a Red Balloon

This method was given to me for relieving headaches. I found it very effective (I don't get them anymore). It can be used for any pain, but can also be used effectively for any unwanted thought or feeling.

Here's how it's done:

1. Feel any unwanted feelings (or pain) in your body.
2. See those areas as bright red energy.
3. Place a bright red balloon around that energy, and tie it with a string.
4. Let it float up and out of your body and mind.
5. Watch it float away, higher and further, getting smaller and smaller, until it is completely out of sight and let go of.

## 14. Allow It to Evaporate

This is another "dissolving" technique.

1. Imagine that your unwanted thoughts and feelings are like water.
2. Allow them to evaporate like steam off hot pavement.
3. As they evaporate, allow yourself to feel the openness their leaving has created.
4. Relax into this openness.

The threat of negative feelings may seem very real, but they are nothing more than mirages, just as heat over sand in a desert or over a roadway may appear as water. They have no real substance. Allow the unwanted feelings to evaporate and dissolve as the mirages that they are.

## 15. Use a Water Valve to Control the Flow

Our suppressed feelings are actually built-up energy (photonic). When this energy builds up, it requires more energy to suppress and manage it (keep it under control). When we release/relieve this pressure, we go through life nice and relaxed.

Here's a way to relieve the pressure:

1. Put your head down and place your hand on your stomach or chest to assist you in *feeling* the sensation of the feeling.
2. Notice the feeling in your body.
3. Rate the feeling on a scale from 0 to 10.
4. See the feeling as water under pressure in your stomach or chest.
5. Mentally imagine a tap or valve over that energy.
6. Open that valve and let the feeling come gushing out.
7. You can open or close this valve as much as you'd like to control the flow.
8. Allow the feelings to be let go of until you are quiet inside.
9. Rate the feeling again on the scale from 0 to 10. Did it lessen? If so, you are heading in the right direction. Keep going until it is zero. If it is not lessening, go back through the steps or try another approach.

## 16. Let Go of Just 1 Percent

Sometimes we feel overwhelmed at the prospect of welcoming up and releasing our suppressed feelings.

Keep in mind that you don't need to let go of every bit of a feeling all at once. Don't let your feelings overwhelm you.

Try this:

1. Notice if the feeling feels too big to let go of.
2. Choose to let go of just 1 percent of whatever is there.
3. Allow 1 percent of the feeling to release (you can just drop it or use any of the other methods in this report).

You'll notice that you'll actually end up letting go of much more than 1 percent of the feeling and will find yourself feeling much lighter and freer.

17. Embrace It with Compassion

Everyone needs love and compassion. Even our feelings do.
Nonlove is what causes all our troubles. Love and compassion
heal all.

Try a compassionate approach to your feelings:

1. Put your head down and place your hand on your stomach
   or chest to assist you in *feeling* the sensation of the feeling.
2. Notice the feeling in your body.
3. Rate the feeling on a scale from 0 to 10.
4. Now, could you embrace the feeling with love and compassion as a mother or father would a child who was in
   pain?
5. Comfort the feeling.
6. Allow yourself to feel one with the pain or discomfort of
   the feeling.
7. As you feel compassion for it, it will lessen more and more
   or dissolve completely.
8. Rate the feeling again on the scale from 0 to 10. Did it
   lessen? If so, you are heading in the right direction. Keep
   going until it is zero. If it is not lessening, go back through
   the steps or try another approach.

---

**Note:** This bonus is provided by Peter Michel and used here with his
kind permission. To get his book, which reveals more than 50 clearing
methods, see www.emotionalfreedom101.com.

# Bibliography

Atkinson, William Walter. *Thought Vibration, or The Law of Attraction in the Thought World.* Chicago: New Thought Publishing, 1906.

Behrend, Genevieve, and Vitale, Joe. *How to Attain Your Desires by Letting Your Subconscious Mind Work for You.* Garden City, NY: Morgan-James Publishing, 2004.

Behrend, Genevieve, and Vitale, Joe. *How to Attain Your Desires,* Vol. 2: *How to Live Life and Love It!* Garden City, NY: Morgan-James Publishing, 2005.

Braden, Gregg. *The Divine Matrix: Bridging Time, Space, Miracles, and Belief.* Carlsbad, CA: Hay House, 2006.

Bristol, Claude. *The Magic of Believing.* New York: Pocket Books, 1991.

Byrne, Rhonda. *The Secret.* New York: Atria Books/Beyond Words, 2006.

Callahan, Roger. *Tapping the Healer Within: Using Thought-Field Therapy to Instantly Conquer Your Fears, Anxieties, and Emotional Distress.* New York: McGraw-Hill, 2002.

Canfield, Jack, with Janet Switzer. *The Success Principles: How to Get from Where You Are to Where You Want to Be.* New York: Harper Collins, 2006.

Casey, Karen. *Change Your Mind and Your Life Will Follow.* New York: Conari Press, 2005.

Coates, Denise. *Feel It Real! The Magical Power of Emotions.* N.p.: Denise Coates Publishers, 2006.

Cornyn-Selby, Alyce. *What's Your Sabotage?* N.p.: Beynch Press, 2000.

Deutschman, Alan. *Change or Die: The Three Keys to Change at Work and in Life.* New York: ReganBooks, 2007.

Di Marsico, Bruce. *The Option Method: Unlock Your Happiness with Five Simple Questions.* Walnut Grove, CA: Dragonfly Press, 2006.

Dwoskin, Hale. *The Sedona Method: Your Key to Lasting Happiness, Success, Peace and Emotional Well-Being.* Sedona, AZ: Sedona Press, 2003.

Eker, T. Harv. *Secrets of the Millionaire Mind: Mastering the Inner Game of Wealth.* New York: Harper Collins, 2005.

Ellsworth, Paul. *Mind Magnet: How to Unify and Intensify Your Natural Faculties for Efficiency, Health and Success*. Holyoke, MA: Elizabeth Towne Company, 1924.

Evans, Mandy. *Travelling Free: How to Recover from the Past*. Encinitas, CA: Yes You Can Press, 2005.

Ford, Debbie. *The Dark Side of the Light Chasers*. New York: RiverHead Books, 1998.

Gage, Randy. *Why You're Dumb, Sick & Broke . . . and How to Get Smart, Healthy & Rich!* Hoboken, NJ: John Wiley & Sons, 2006.

Gilmore, Ehryck. *The Law of Attraction 101*. Chicago: Eromlig Publishing, 2006.

Goddard, Neville. *Immortal Man: A Compilation of Lectures*. Camarillo, CA: DeVorss & Company, 1999.

Goddard, Neville. *The Law and the Promise*. Camarillo, CA: DeVorss & Company, 1984.

Goddard, Neville. *The Power of Awareness*. Camarillo, CA: DeVorss & Company, 1983.

Goddard, Neville. *Your Faith Is Your Fortune*. Camarillo, CA: DeVorss & Company, 1985.

Goddard, Neville and Joe Vitale. *At Your Command*. Garden City, NY: Morgan-James Publishing, 2005.

Goldberg, Bruce. *Karmic Capitalism: A Spiritual Approach to Financial Independence*. Baltimore, MD: Publish America, 2005.

Harris, Bill. *Thresholds of the Mind: Your Personal Roadmap to Success, Happiness, and Contentment*. Beaverton, OR: Centerpoint Research, 2002.

Hawkins, David. *Devotional Nonduality*. Sedona, AZ: Veritas Publishing, 2006.

Hawkins, David. *I: Reality and Subjectivity*. Sedona, AZ: Veritas Publishing, 2003.

Hawkins, David. *Transcending the Levels of Consciousness*. Sedona, AZ: Veritas Publishing, 2006.

Hicks, Jerry, and Esther Hicks. *Ask and It Is Given: Learning to Manifest Your Desires*. Carlsbad, CA: Hay House, 2004.

Hicks, Jerry, and Esther Hicks. *The Law of Attraction: The Basics of the Teachings of Abraham*. Carlsbad, CA: Hay House, 2006.

Hogan, Kevin. *The Science of Influence*. Hoboken, NJ: John Wiley & Sons, 2004.

Holmes, Ernest. *Science of Mind*. New York: Tarcher, 1998.

Joyner, Mark. *Simpleology: The Simple Science of Getting What You Want*. Hoboken, NJ: John Wiley & Sons, 2007.

Kaa, Sri Ram. *2012: You Have a Choice!* Tijeras, NM: TOSA Publishing, 2006.

Kaufman, Barry Neil. *To Love Is to Be Happy With*. New York: Fawcett, 1985.

Kennedy, Dan. *No B.S. Wealth Attraction for Entrepreneurs*. N.p.: Entrepreneur Press, 2006.

Kristof, Aziz. *The Human Buddha: Enlightenment for the New Millennium*. New Delhi, India: Kristof, 2006.

Landrum, Gene. *The Superman Syndrome: The Magic of Myth in the Pursuit of Power; The Positive Mental Moxie of Myth for Personal Growth*. N.p.: iUniverse, 2005.

Lapin, Rabbi Daniel. *Thou Shall Prosper: Ten Commandments for Making Money*. Hoboken, NJ: John Wiley & Sons, 2002.

Larson, Christian D. *Your Forces and How to Use Them*. London: Fowler, 1912.

Larson, Melody. *The Beginner's Guide to Abundance*. N.p.: Booklocker.com, 2007.

Levenson, Lester. *No Attachments, No Aversions: The Autobiography of a Master*. Sherman Oaks, CA: Lawrence Crane Enterprises, 2003.

Levenson, Lester. *The Ultimate Truth about Love & Happiness: A Handbook for Life*. Sherman Oaks, CA: Lawrence Crane Enterprises, 2003.

Lipton, Bruce. *The Biology of Belief: Unleashing the Power of Consciousness, Matter and Miracles*. N.p.: Mountain of Love, 2005.

Losier, Michael. *Law of Attraction*. Victoria, Canada: Losier Publications, 2003.

McTaggart, Lynne. *The Intention Experiment: Using Your Thoughts to Change Your Life and the World*. New York: Free Press, 2007.

Oates, Robert. *Permanent Peace*. Institute of Science, Technology and Public Policy, 2002.

Ponder, Catherine. *The Dynamic Laws of Prosperity*. Camarillo, CA: DeVorss & Company, 1985.

Proctor, Bob. *You Were Born Rich: Now You Can Discover and Develop Those Riches.* Toronto, Canada: LifeSuccess Productions, 1997.

Ray, James Arthur. *The Science of Success: How to Attract Prosperity and Create Harmonic Wealth through Proven Principles.* N.p.: Sun Ark Press, 1999.

Ressler, Peter, and Monika Mitchell Ressler. *Spiritual Capitalism: How 9/11 Gave Us Nine Spiritual Lessons of Work and Business.* New York: Chilmark Books, 2007.

Ringer, Robert. *Looking Out for 1.* New York: Fawcett, 1985.

Ringer, Robert. *Winning Through Intimidation.* New York: Fawcett, 1984.

Scheinfeld, Robert. *Busting Loose from the Money Game: Mind-Blowing Strategies for Changing the Rules of a Game You Can't Win.* Hoboken, NJ: John Wiley & Sons, 2006.

Shumsky, Susan. *Miracle Prayer: Nine Steps to Creating Prayers that Get Results.* Berkeley, CA: Celestial Arts, 2006.

Sugarman, Joseph. *Triggers.* Las Vegas, NV: Delstar Publishing, 1999.

Tipping, Colin. *Radical Forgiveness: Making Room for the Miracle.* Marietta, GA: Global 13 Publications, 2002.

Tipping, Colin. *Radical Manifestation: The Fine Art of Creating the Life You Want.* Marietta, GA: Global 13 Publications, 2006.

Vitale, Joe. *Adventures Within: Confessions of an Inner World Journalist.* N.p.: AuthorHouse, 2003.

Vitale, Joe. *The Attractor Factor: Five Easy Steps for Creating Wealth (or Anything Else) from the Inside Out.* Hoboken, NJ: John Wiley & Sons, 2005.

Vitale, Joe. *Buying Trances: A New Psychology of Sales and Marketing.* Hoboken, NJ: John Wiley & Sons, 2007.

Vitale, Joe. *The Greatest Money-Making Secret in History.* N.p.: 1st Books Library, 2003.

Vitale, Joe. *Hypnotic Writing.* Hoboken, NJ: John Wiley & Sons, 2007.

Vitale, Joe. *Life's Missing Instruction Manual: The Guidebook You Should Have Been Given at Birth.* Hoboken, NJ: John Wiley & Sons, 2006.

Vitale, Joe. *The Seven Lost Secrets of Success*. Hoboken, NJ: John Wiley & Sons, 2007.

Vitale, Joe. *There's a Customer Born Every Minute: P.T. Barnum's Amazing 10 "Rings of Power" for Creating Fame, Fortune, and a Business Empire Today—Guaranteed!* Hoboken, NJ: John Wiley & Sons, 2006.

Vitale, Joe, and Ihaleakala Hew Len. *Zero Limits: The Secret Hawaiian System for Wealth, Health, Peace, and More*. Hoboken, NJ: John Wiley & Sons, 2007.

Vitale, Joe, and Bill Hibbler. *Meet and Grow Rich*. Hoboken, NJ: John Wiley & Sons, 2006.

Wattles, Wallace D. *How to Get What You Want*. Publisher unknown.

Wattles, Wallace D. *The Science of Getting Rich*. New York: Penguin/ Tarcher, 2007.

Wilber, Ken. *Quantum Questions: Mystical Writings of the World's Greatest Physicists*. Boston: Shambhala, 2001.

Wojton, Djuna. *Karmic Healing: Clearing Past-Life Blocks to Present-Day Love, Health, and Happiness*. Berkeley, CA: Crossing Press, 2006.

# About the Author

One of the stars of the movie *The Secret*, Dr. Joe Vitale is president of Hypnotic Marketing, Inc., and president of Frontier Nutritional Research, Inc., both companies based outside of Austin, Texas.

He is the author of way too many books to list here, including the #1 best-selling book *The Attractor Factor*, the #1 best seller *Life's Missing Instruction Manual*, and the best-selling Nightingale-Conant audioprogram, *The Power of Outrageous Marketing*.

He has also written *The E-Code, There's a Customer Born Every Minute, The Seven Lost Secrets of Success, Hypnotic Writing, Your Internet Cash Machine*, and *Buying Trances*, and is co-author of *Meet and Grow Rich* and *Zero Limits*, all published by John Wiley & Sons.

Once homeless and living in poverty, Joe is now considered one of the pioneers of Internet marketing. He has helped people become millionaires and has helped create online empires.

Due to his work in *The Secret* and to the success of his books *The Attractor Factor* and *Zero Limits*, he is now becoming known as a self-help guru. He's often called the Buddha of the Internet.

His main web site is at www.mrfire.com.

*Special Offer*

*Who Else Wants a Miracles Coach?*
**Finally Overcome the Internal Roadblocks That Prevent You from Attracting the Results You Want with the Help of Dr. Joe Vitale's Miracles Coaching Program.**

You need to be *clear* to achieve the results you want. If there are any counter-intentions within you, consciously or unconsciously, you will not attract the results you really want. If you do achieve them, they will be temporary and you will lose them.

So, how do you get clear? How do you get rid of the roadblocks and go warp speed ahead, right to whatever it is you're trying to attract?

You can use the 10 methods in this book, but if you want even faster results and/or you want some personal direction, you may need a Miracles Coach. For a limited time, you can apply to be mentored at the Miracles Coaching web site.

For details, see www.miraclescoaching.com.

*The cause of success is not in the environment of the individual, because if it were, all persons within a given radius would be successful, and success would be wholly a matter of neighborhood; and we see that people whose environments are practically the same and who live in the same neighborhood show us all degrees of success and failure; therefore, we know that the cause of success must be in the individual, and nowhere else.*

—Wallace D. Wattles, author of *How to Get What You Want* and *The Science of Getting Rich*

# Index